THE WRECKS OF

Chris Michael

LIVERPOOL MARINE PRESS

Published by Liverpool Marine Press, 11 Graham Road, Merseyside L48 5DN

Typeset by the author and printed by Saints Printers, Liverpool

ISBN 0 9524315 0 5

Front cover design by David Michael showing the *Ocean Monarch* on fire.

Contents

Acknowledgements

I have been very pleased to obtain first hand reports from some of those who were witnesses of some of the losses described: Captain F. H. Simpson, Captain J. Hoffman, Harry Shakeshaft, Captain M. White, Mr. S. C. Heal and Mike Dobson. Many thanks also for advice from Mr. Hollingwood, Mr. G. Meachim, Sid Lindsay, John Hughes, Ian Stockbridge and Dr. C. V. Waine. I thank the staff of Liverpool City Library, the Guildhall Library and the Merseyside Maritime Museum. I appreciate the help of fellow divers who have been most generous with information and advice: especially Chris Holden, Keith Hurley, Geoff Oldfield, Dave Huggins, Simon Rodger and my colleagues from the Liverpool University Sub Aqua Club. I acknowledge useful information from charter boat skippers: John Povah, Alan Price and Eddy Ward.

I thank those who have provided me with photographs or drawings: Mr. Hollingwood, Mr. G. Meachim, Gordon Tufnell, Sid Lindsay and R. Hubens the archivist of Geytenbeek. I thank Tony Tollitt for help with photographic work. I acknowledge permission to reproduce photographs from the Trustees of the National Museums and Galleries on Merseyside (Merseyside Maritime Museum) (p 11, 29b, 33, 37, 41, 43a, 45a, 69b); National Maritime Museum London (p 7, 29a); John Clarkson, Longton (p 49a, 55, 69a); Illustrated London News (p 17, 23); Hull Museum (p 53a); World Ship Photographic Library (p 71a); and Gordon Tufnell (p 71b). For several illustrations, I have been unable to establish copyright and I apologise in advance if any omission has occurred.

While I have tried to be as accurate as possible, due caution should be exercised by anyone attempting dives on any site described in this book. Please let me know if you discover any errors or inaccuracies in this book. I should also be grateful to receive any relevant information about shipwrecks in Liverpool Bay. In particular I should like to hear about photographs or postcards of any wreck. I can be contacted through my publisher.

Chris Michael
1994

Chapter 1

Introduction

Hundreds of wrecks have occurred in the sea area around Liverpool. The tragedy of shipwreck and the heroism of individual seamen comes across forcefully in the records of these losses. An insight into the nature and importance of the shipping using the Port of Liverpool across the years can be obtained from the stories of the vessels wrecked. I shall try to tell the true tale of as many of these shipwrecks as I can. My interest in the wrecks of Liverpool Bay arose because I am a keen amateur diver living on Merseyside. I have dived on the remains of many of the wrecks and I describe the present state of the wreckage and the marine life to be found around the wrecks.

The Mersey and Dee estuaries provide natural shelter to shipping and are strategically placed on the west coast of England. The ports of this area have been important for many centuries. With a high volume of shipping, it is not surprising that disasters were frequent. Many of the wrecks occurred as vessels were swept onto the sandbanks that surround the shipping channels to the ports. These wrecks have mostly been dispersed by storms and covered by the shifting sands. The wrecks in deeper water in the approaches to Liverpool have been better preserved and it is these on which I shall concentrate. A map of the locations of many of these wrecks is provided. Deeper water wrecks could be caused by severe weather swamping a vessel but other causes such as fire, collision, bombs and mines also took their toll.

Liverpool was one of the main ports for emigrants to America. Two transatlantic passenger vessels met their fate in Liverpool Bay. The sailing packet *Ocean Monarch* caught fire on her outward journey in 1848 with huge loss of life. On her return journey in 1883 the *City of Brussels* sank after a collision in fog. She had been a crack liner in her time - a Blue Riband holder. The location of both of these historic wrecks is known and provides further information about the ships themselves.

One of the episodes in the history of the Mersey that has caught many people's imagination is the support given by Liverpool to the Confederate cause at the time of the American Civil War. This support arose from trading links - particularly

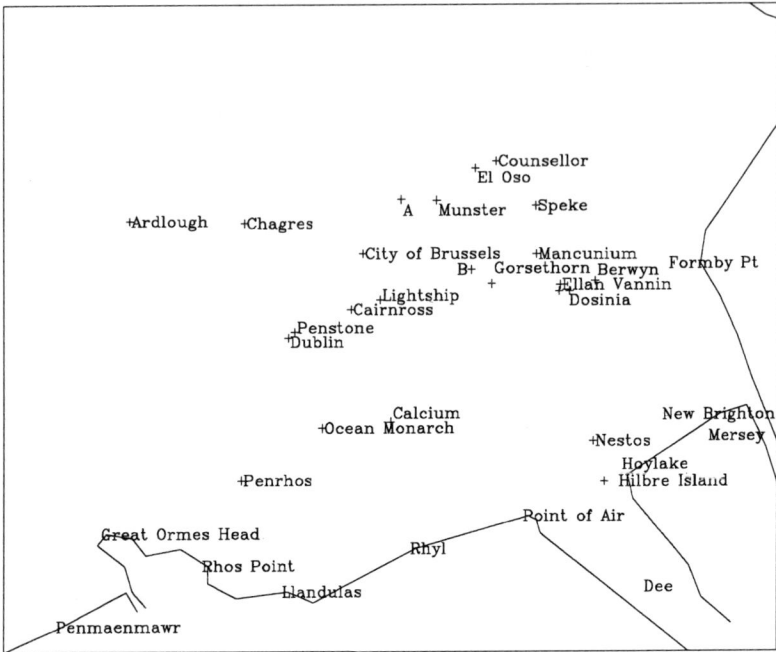

The location of wrecks in Liverpool Bay

through the import of cotton from the Southern States. At the time of the Civil War, Confederate agents arranged to have ships built on the Mersey. The *Alabama* is best known because of its naval battles. Other vessels were built as blockade carriers - fast vessels of shallow draught which could get into the blockaded Southern ports to bring out the valuable cotton as cargo. One such vessel was the *Lelia*. She was built in Toxteth and was nominally in British hands when she left the Mersey in 1865. The intention was to transfer ownership at sea. This scheme never came to pass because she was unable to cope with heavy weather in Liverpool Bay. There was a heavy loss of life, compounded by more lives lost in a Liverpool Lifeboat that set out to render assistance. This sorry saga is described in detail. The location of the wreck of the *Lelia* is not definitely known, though I discuss possible sites. There is great interest among divers to locate her.

Another incredible episode in Mersey ship building was the construction of the first steam powered submarine, the *Resurgam*. She was designed by a Liverpool inventor, the Reverend George Garrett. The story of her construction and trials is amazing. She was being taken by sea to Portsmouth to be demonstrated to the

Navy when she was lost in Liverpool Bay. Her precise location is unknown and considerable efforts have already been made to locate the historic wreck. I give what guidance I can as to her whereabouts. Another submarine incident was much more tragic. The *Thetis* sank during trials in Liverpool Bay in 1936 ending up with her bow on the seabed but with her stern sticking out of the water. Those inside could be heard knocking but could not be rescued in time. Only 4 men escaped. The vessel was eventually beached on Anglesey and was put back in service. So, in this case, there is no wreckage in Liverpool Bay.

The Dee and, more recently, Liverpool have served as the natural ferry ports for Ireland. Liverpool has also been closely linked to the Isle of Man. Wrecks of passenger ferries give rise to strong emotions - probably because they are the only type of ship that most people ever experience. There have been several wrecks of Irish Sea ferries in Liverpool Bay. The earliest wreck was only brought to light when divers recovered the bell of the *Dublin* from a wreck which was previously unidentified. The *Dublin* was a Liverpool - Dublin ferry belonging to the Tedcastle Line. She was sunk by a collision with the *Longford* which was providing a ferry service for the rival City of Dublin Steam Packet Company. Fortunately there was no loss of life. A much more tragic loss was that of the Isle of Man ferry *Ellan Vannin*. Her plight was publicised by the song performed by the Spinners folk group. The full story is recounted later. The third ferry loss was that of the incoming Belfast ferry *Munster* which was mined in 1940. All the passengers and crew were rescued with no loss of life: the detailed story is presented.

The importance of Liverpool as a destination for trans-atlantic convoys in the last war made the nearby shipping lanes a target for mines, torpedoes and bombing. Huge losses resulted. In the first few months of 1940, no fewer than 5 large steamships were sunk by mines in Liverpool Bay. When an effective defence against magnetic mines had been established, the rate of loss was considerably reduced. In the early months of the War, the newspapers carried details of the losses and of the heroism of individual seamen. Later, the censor struck and only allowed the publication of the total tonnage of vessels lost each month. In some cases, I have been able to get first hand accounts from crew members serving on these vessels when they were mined. A clearer picture is now available of the drama of these losses.

As well as the convoys whose contribution was widely appreciated, a very important part of the War effort was played by the coasters that distributed cargo around the coast of Britain. They travelled alone with at most a small gun for protection. The shipping marks were dimly lit and they travelled routes sometimes unswept by minesweepers. The losses of 6 vessels are described. Some of these smaller vessels lie fairly intact on the seabed. In one case, the *Speke*, the present state of the wreckage clarifies the mystery surrounding her disappearance.

Another wreck which has been identified by divers is the Lightship *Alarm*. This is a fairly intact lightship which sank after a collision in 1911. Other miscellaneous wreckage in Liverpool Bay includes the remains of 3 Wartime Anti Aircraft Forts. There are several charted shipwrecks where the identity of the vessel is unknown. I discuss the present state of the underwater wreckage as a guide to identifying the vessel.

Despite modern safety equipment, shipwrecks still occur in Liverpool Bay. The most recent sinking was the *Ardlough* in 1988. The stories of the loss of the *Berwyn* and *Penstone* are also told.

The wrecks of Liverpool Bay are justifiably popular with wreck fishermen. One would expect Liverpool Bay to be a popular dive destination too, but there are plenty of wrecks at reasonable depths which have rarely been dived. The reasons for this lack of dive saturation are in part that diving in Liverpool Bay can be difficult. The Bay is exposed to the prevailing winds and has strong currents. The visibility under water can be poor. The wrecks further out have better visibility but need longer boat journeys and good navigation to find them. Nevertheless, some very exciting and stimulating diving awaits the adventurous - and I give information to help other divers locate and enjoy these wrecks.

Chapter 2

Emigrant Ships

Liverpool was one of the main ports for emigrants to America. With the coming of the railway to Liverpool, it was more convenient for European emigrants to use Liverpool on the west coast of Britain as a departure point. Regular services were run - even in the days of sail - from the 1820's. These were the first transatlantic liners. The main difficulty lay in the westbound crossing into the prevailing winds. Typically this took 34 days compared to an average of 22 days for the eastbound return leg. These crossing times were much improved upon by the early steamships which averaged 17 days westbound and 15 days eastbound. For those passengers able to pay for a cabin passage, the steamships were a much better proposition and they dominated this trade from the 1840's. The sailing ships competed in the bargain basement. They took increasing numbers of steerage passengers - often 400 at a time compared to 40 or less cabin passengers taken in earlier days. Life on board a west bound sailing packet for the steerage passengers was pretty tough. One such vessel was the *Ocean Monarch* which met her fate with great loss of life when fire broke out soon after leaving Liverpool.

With the coming of steam, different companies competed to obtain the fastest crossing. The Inman line was one of the early steamship lines. To increase the speed of their ships, they ordered screw vessels that were longer and narrower. Their *City of Paris* was the first screw liner able to beat the crossing times of the Cunard paddle steamer *Scotia*. The *City of Brussels* was built to capitalise on this success. Although there was a great demand by passengers for the westbound voyage, the eastbound ships were usually not fully loaded. On one such eastbound voyage, the *City of Brussels* collided in fog with another vessel in Liverpool Bay and sank with some loss of life.

The location of both of these wrecks is known and they are often dived. This provides further information about the ships themselves.

Ocean Monarch

American passenger liner (sail) 1301 tons gross, 179 ft long, 40 ft beam, 27 ft draught.
Built: Donald McKay, USA, 1843.
Owners: E. Train & Co.(White Diamond Line), registered at Boston.
Date of wreck: 24 Aug 1848
Location: 53^0 25.40' N 3^0 35.37' W
Distance from New Brighton: 20 nautical miles.
Depth at low water: 17m seabed, no scour, 15m to top of wreck.

By 1848, steamships were carrying around half of the transatlantic passenger trade. Sailing ships were usually almost as fast eastwards but took twice as long on the westbound crossing. Even so, sailing ships were able to provide a regular service in competition. Enoch Train and Company's White Diamond Line ran a weekly Liverpool to Boston service. To attract passengers, they advertised through bookings by rail from Boston to various American cities. Their fleet of ships had the reputation of being well built and, though not especially fast, of being able to keep up a good speed in foul weather.

More and more of the cabin passengers preferred the reliability and speed of steam, so the emigrants travelling steerage were sought by the sailing packets to make good the lost cabin passengers. Life in steerage on an ocean crossing of 30 days or more was uncomfortable. The steerage passengers were packed into accommodation below decks and allocated a wooden box to sleep in. The sleeping accommodation was segregated into male and female. They were only allowed up on deck for short periods each day. On sailing ships they were not served with cooked meals. Basic supplies of tea, porridge and biscuits were provided as well as cooking places. They were expected to bring extra food, a straw mattress, plates and (on some ships) a chamber pot.

The *Ocean Monarch* left Liverpool early on the morning of Thursday 24 August. She had 396 people aboard, of whom 322 were steerage passengers. She had 32 cabin passengers and 42 crew. Her cargo was iron, dry goods, salt and earthenware. The earthenware was packed in crates stuffed with straw. She was towed out by a steam tug and at about 8.00 am, she set off under sail in a fresh breeze. Nothing of any consequence happened until about midday when she was 6 miles short of Great Ormes Head.

Smoke was discovered in one of the aft cabins. Despite attempts to put the fire out with buckets of water, it spread quickly. The ship was steered downwind to try to lessen the apparent wind but this just resulted in smoke getting everywhere. This caused confusion among the passengers. As panic broke out, Captain Murdock ordered the two anchors to be released to bring her bow up wind. The passengers crowded forward and onto the bowsprit to distance themselves from the flames astern. Many jumped overboard and, although a few caught hold of floating

The *Ocean Monarch* on fire in Liverpool Bay. The Brazilian steam frigate *Affonso* is on the right and the yacht *Queen of the South* is in the centre.

wooden objects, many drowned. The captain had difficulty giving orders amid all the screams. He ordered the boats to be lowered and two were successfully launched. The rest were engulfed in flames. The wooden topgallant yard was cut down and held alongside with a rope so people could cling to it when they jumped overboard.

The sad tragedy unfolding was seen by several boats in the vicinity. The first to arrive was the yacht *Queen of the South*. This belonged to Mr. Littledale who was Commodore of the Royal Mersey Yacht Club and who was returning from a regatta at Beaumaris. He and his crew managed to save 32 people. The scene which he witnessed was most appalling and harrowing. Flames were bursting furiously from the stern and centre of the vessel. To escape them, the passengers crowded in the fore part. Some jumped overboard and were not seen again. In turn the mizzenmast and then the mainmast went overboard. The foremast still stood. As the fire crept forward, the passengers and crew were forced forward too. They clung to the jib boom in clusters - even one lying on top of another. At length the foremast went overboard which snapped the fastenings of the jib boom. This boom with its load of humanity then dropped into the water amidst the most heart rending screams. Some regained the vessel or a floating spar but many were lost.

The next vessel to assist was the Brazilian steam frigate *Affonso* which was out on a pleasure excursion. She was commanded by Captain Lisboa and had on board the Prince of Joinville, the Duke d'Aumale, the Brazilian Minister the Chevalier de Lisboa, Admiral Grenville and their parties among other distinguished persons. She was able to anchor close by and lower 4 boats to pick up survivors. About 160 were rescued and received attention aboard the *Affonso*.

Another vessel lending assistance was the Bangor bound steamer *Prince of Wales*. She and the American ship *New World* used their boats to pick up survivors clinging to floating wreckage. Towards the end of this tragic affair, there were only a few helpless women and children left on the wreck. They were paralysed with fear and unable to get down from the tottering bowsprit into the waiting boats. They were saved by an act of heroism by Frederick Jerome who stripped and swam to the wreck with a line in his hand. He succeeded in lowering the last victims to safety and was himself the last to leave the wreck. Mr. Jerome was a sailor on the American ship *New World* but was British, having been born in Portsmouth. He had previously shown courage in an incident when the packet ship *Henry Clay* was stranded near New York.

Not all assistance was so selfless and there are contemporary reports of passengers in one of the *Ocean Monarch's* boats who were picked up by a Chester pilot boat *Pilot Queen* and robbed. Then they were returned to their boat while the *Pilot Queen* went back to the wreck scene to look for more valuables, such as floating trunks.

The *Ocean Monarch* continued to burn until the flames got down to the water line. Apart from the figurehead which was intact, she looked as if she had been neatly cut a few inches above the water. In fine calm weather, she sank at anchor during the night. There was a hissing and cracking sound as the flames were extinguished and she slid beneath the waves, stern first. The figurehead floated off and was eventually recovered at Rhos and used to decorate a wall in a hotel.

The loss of the *Ocean Monarch* was one of the worst disasters that occurred to emigrant ships. In total 178 lives were lost. Various reasons for the fire were claimed - that pipe smoking passengers were responsible, that careless use of a candle by the crew was responsible,..

A collection was made to assist the survivors and a considerable sum was donated. Awards were made by the Liverpool Shipwreck and Humane Society to the rescuers: to Mr. Littledale and the crew of his yacht, to Admiral Grenfell and Captain Lisboa, and to Frederick Jerome. Although the Prince of Joinville is said to have given succour to the afflicted when brought aboard the *Affonso*, he also found time to sketch the tragedy. This picture graphically tells the dreadful tale.

The wreck site is assumed to be the *Ocean Monarch*. She is marked as 'position approximate' on the chart with the position given above. I estimate that her true position is closer to 53^0 25.35' N 3^0 35.58' W. The wreck was originally found from information obtained by a trawler that caught her nets on an underwater obstruction. The wreck is apparently on an even keel but only a metre or two above the level of the surrounding seabed. She lies north - south and appears to be of wood with iron cylinders scattered around. There is some coarse fishing net caught on one side. The wreck was salvaged a few years ago without any treasure being recovered. The main feature of note is the amount of pottery to be found. Indeed this site is known locally as the 'plate wreck'. This wreck is a 'Conger City'. Every crack seems to have its resident mean grin. I have seen a dozen congers during one dive.

City of Brussels

Passenger liner (steam) 3775 tons gross, 390 ft long, 40 ft beam, 34 ft draught.
Built: Tod & McGregor, Glasgow 1869.
Engines: Steam Compound with 4 cylinders giving 500 hp, built by Laird Bros., Birkenhead, one screw.
Owners: Inman Line, registered Liverpool.
Date of wreck: 7 Jan 1883
Location: 53^0 33.48' N 3^0 32.18' W
Distance from New Brighton: 19 nautical miles.
Depth at low water: 24m seabed, 25m scour, 17m to top of wreck.

The *City of Brussels* was a crack transatlantic liner. Her owners, the Inman line, were strong competitors for transatlantic trade. They ordered the *City of Brussels* with the intention of capturing the Blue Riband for the fastest crossing. She was designed with a length to width ratio of 10 which was greater than the values of 8 or so common previously: a long thin fast boat by the standards of the time. She had accommodation for 200 cabin and 600 steerage passengers. She was also the first transatlantic liner to have steam steering gear - this was constructed by the Vauxhall Foundry in Liverpool. Her fuel consumption was 110 tons of coal a day.

She entered service in October 1869 and made the fastest crossing up to that date in December from New York to Queenstown (now named Cobh) with an average speed of 14.66 knots. This took the record from the Cunard Company's *Russia*.

In 1876, she was re-engined with compound engines which cut her coal consumption to 65 tons a day. Also a promenade deck and a second funnel were added. She could now accommodate 1000 steerage passengers. She had already had mishaps - twice breaking her mainshaft in mid-ocean when thousands were kept in painful suspense for weeks while she continued slowly under sail.

In early 1883 she was inbound from New York with 70 passengers and 97 crew under the command of Captain Land. In thick fog she reduced speed to half and then to dead slow. Another vessel's siren was heard. She was stationary when that other vessel's bows struck her on her own starboard bow, cutting through to the waterline. Even though it was 5.30 in the morning and most passengers were asleep, there was no panic and the boats were lowered. The majority of the passengers and crew were taken aboard the *Kirby Hall* which was the vessel she had collided with. The *Kirby Hall* of the Hall Line was a large steamship on her maiden voyage to India. Two Italian steerage passengers and 8 crew were lost from the *City of Brussels*.

The *City of Brussels* is the most dived wreck in Liverpool Bay. She is reasonably intact around the counter stern which is the highest part of the wreck and lies to the east. Nearby lie engine components and further west are the scattered bow sections. As a passenger ship, she had opulent fittings and there is always hope of finding a nice souvenir among the wreckage. The visibility is usually relatively good and there is plenty of marine life - including large fish: pollack and ling.

The *City of Brussels* before she was re-engined.

Chapter 3

Confederate Ships

By 1864, the blockade of the Confederate States by the United States Navy was very effective. The Southern states could not get their cotton out to earn money, and they could not get coal, iron or weapons in. To counter this blockade, the Confederate States sought to obtain suitable ships. Liverpool was one of the main ports to import cotton from the Southern States of America. The strong links lead Confederate agents to place orders for ships to be built on the Mersey. These vessels were often ordered in the name of a British nominee and were to be paid for by future cotton imports. To deal with this blockade, two classes of vessel were sought.

The most ambitious plan was the attempt to obtain warships. Because of international law, Confederate warships, as such, could not be built in Britain. The way to get round this restriction was to build the basic vessel with great strength in Britain and then fit her out with guns in some foreign port. This attempt by the Confederacy to combat the great power of the US fleet was very dramatic but eventually doomed. The *Alabama* was such a warship which was built by Lairds on the Mersey in 1862. Her role was to harass US shipping and during two years she managed to sink 68 merchant ships. She was eventually discovered undergoing repairs at Cherbourg by the USS *Kearsage*. The *Kearsage* waited off Cherbourg and forced the *Alabama* to engage in battle on 19 June 1864. It was quite an even battle with both ships inflicting heavy damage. The damage caused to the *Alabama* was sufficient to sink her and her wreckage lies off the coast of France. Subsequent vessels, such as the iron steam rams being built by Lairds, were prevented by the British Government from being delivered.

Other vessels were built as blockade carriers - fast vessels of shallow draught which could get into the blockaded Southern ports to bring out the valuable cotton as cargo. They needed to carry enough coal for a few days steaming at high speed to get them through the blockades but otherwise relied on sail. The best design proved to be paddle steamers of cast steel over 200 ft in length with powerful engines. There were about 14 such ships on order in various British shipyards. Liverpool was foremost in producing these vessels and in January 1865 four blockade runners were launched on the same day from the yard of Jones, Quiggin & Co. Though the overall responsibility lay with General McRae of the Confederate Navy, the ships were ordered by agents.

The newly built vessels could not leave Britain with war material on board but could pick up such supplies at Bermuda on the way out. Even though these vessels were not designed as warships, it was envisaged that they could be fitted with a few guns and make brief sallies from a blockaded port to try and attack the blockading fleet. The blockade runners were mainly intended to trade from Southern ports such as Wilmington only as far as Bermuda with their cargo, but they had to be capable of crossing the Atlantic under sail on delivery. One such vessel was the *Lelia*. She was built in Toxteth and was nominally in British hands when she left the Mersey in 1865. The intention was to transfer ownership at sea. There seems to have been a desperate rush to send her across the Atlantic. She left in bad weather and with her equipment not fully in place. She proved unable to cope with stormy weather in Liverpool Bay. There was a heavy loss of life, compounded by more lives lost in a Liverpool Lifeboat that set out to render assistance.

The location of the wreck of the *Lelia* is not definitely known though she was a big enough vessel that substantial remains must await the adventurous diver. I give what clues there are about her possible location.

Lelia

Confederate steamship 640 tons gross, 252 ft long, 30 ft beam, 12 ft draught.
Built: W. C. Miller and Sons, Liverpool 1864.
Engines: Compound diagonal steam, 4 boilers, 300 nhp, paddles, built Fawcett and Preston 1864.
Date of wreck: 14 Jan 1865

One of the blockade runners was built in 1864 by Miller and Sons in their Toxteth yard at Liverpool. Her name *Lelia* was that of the wife of Commander Arthur Sinclair, the Confederate Naval Officer who was in charge of supervising her completion. She was an iron paddle steamer with two compound diagonal steam engines for high speed. With 4 boilers and two funnels, she was capable of 14 knots. The *Lelia* was clipper built and schooner rigged. Her construction comprised one deck with only a forward deck house and a bridge built above it. She carried a cargo of 85 tons and 460 tons of coal. The cargo was 40 tons of iron in her fore hold with the remainder and general hardware in the aft hold. Her bunkers held 340 tons of coal for ship's use and the remaining 120 tons of coal were in the hold. She had just completed her first trial and was on her maiden voyage. Many of the ship's stores had only just been delivered and were not yet put in place. The builder, Mr. Thomas Miller, was on board.

She left Liverpool on 14 January 1865 nominally under the command of Captain Thomas Buckston Skinner and registered as British. Commander Sinclair was aboard and would arrange a transfer of ownership and command en route. She had two pilots aboard, a Liverpool and a Cork pilot and it was intended that the pilots together with two gentlemen, Mr. Thomas Miller and Mr. James Clarke would leave the ship at Holyhead and return by steam tug to Liverpool. Six more gentlemen would continue to her declared destination of Bermuda, one of these being Commander Sinclair. There were 49 crew. The weather was bad and getting worse. By the time she reached the Crosby Lightship there was a strong gale from the North West. Perhaps the urgency of bringing help to the Confederate cause was allowed to overcome nautical common sense.

As she proceeded the weather deteriorated and waves broke over her bows. Her fore deck was constantly being filled with water. When she was near Great Ormes Head, the decision was made to turn back to Liverpool. Although reports in the press suggest that the initial trouble arose from anchors inadequately stowed, the inquiry was presented with evidence that the problem arose from water surging up through the hawse pipes. These were the pipes allowing the anchor chain to pass from the deck outboard. Although the builders supplied chokes to block off these pipes, they were not fitted. So as she buried her head in the waves, she shipped seas through these hawse pipes. This water was then trapped between the forecastle or deckhouse and the stem and broke the bulkhead so getting into the deckhouse. This caused the crew's effects and berths to be washed out and overboard. She was shipping a lot of water which was running around her decks and quite a lot was getting below. This caused her head to be lower in the water which aggravated matters. Pumps were manned forward but the water was pumped onto the deck where it added to the problem. It became progressively harder for the crew to remain forward as seas broke over her. Keys to the sluices that allowed the steam pump to be used were not readily available.

Heading back to Liverpool, she ran at about $7\frac{1}{2}$ knots before the wind for over an hour before broaching in a heavy sea. Her foretopmast staysail was blown away and the carpenter was washed overboard when trying to retrieve bedding. With the foresail hoisted she got going again at about half speed until about 3 or 4 miles west of the North West Lightship. She continued more upwind until abreast of the North West Lightship and about 4 or 5 miles away from it. It was here that the hatches burst from pressure of water below. The crew were all aft and the Captain gave orders to lower the boats at about 5 pm.

Two boats were got away safely but the other two filled and capsized. Despite a lack of rowlocks in the boats, the 30 survivors managed to get near the North West Lightship which must have been down wind. Here one of the boats capsized and all on board were thrown into the water. Only 12 men eventually got safely on board the Lightship. The remaining 47 crew, pilots and gentlemen were lost. The survivors were the boatswain and steward, the engineer's storekeeper, five firemen and four sailors. It is their evidence to a Board of Trade Enquiry which gives us the preceding details.

Some possibility of assistance to the *Lelia* in her plight was available. She flew a distress signal and an outward bound steamer, the *Sovereign*, turned to come to her. Although the *Lelia* slowed her engines, she was still travelling quite fast towards Liverpool and the *Sovereign* turned away again. She also carried two small signal guns but these were not used.

The next morning, the tug *Blazer* saw the signal from the Lightship but was unable to assist because of the cross seas. She returned to Liverpool and took a lifeboat in tow with 11 men aboard. Off the East Hoyle sandbank, the lifeboat capsized. The men in the lifeboat had not taken the precaution of putting their lifebelts on. Only 4 were saved and 7 men were drowned.

Those on the Lightship were picked up the next day by which time the gale had abated somewhat. In total 59 persons were lost. The decomposed body of Commander Arthur Sinclair was picked up by a Fleetwood trawler several months later. It was identified by the gold items and a valuable watch which had stopped at 4.10. Thus ended a tragic attempt to support the Confederate cause.

In 1865, the North West Lightship was anchored approximately 8 miles north of Point of Air. The wind was NW and the above report suggests that the *Lelia* was abandoned upwind of the Lightship. On the day of her loss, high water was at midday so she was abandoned just before low water. After low water, the current would tend to push her towards Liverpool. Thus it is possible that her wreckage is near the present position of the Bar Light. Indeed, as discussed in the section on Miscellaneous Wrecks, there is a wreck 'Unknown B' near the Bar which could well be the *Lelia*. This wreck is on its side and rather sanded in with only the starboard side sticking out of the sea bed.

Although it is important to establish definitely the location of the wreck of the *Lelia*, the wreckage of other confederate blockade runners has been explored. One similar vessel, the *Iona II*, was wrecked on 2 January 1864 just east of Lundy in the Bristol Channel. She was a fast steam blockade runner of 245 feet in length which had been built in Glasgow. She was lost in a collision in fog but the precise location of the wreck was not known at the time. Divers found her wreckage by chance - since she lies close to a more modern wreck, the *Robert*. I have dived the *Iona II* and apart from 4 impressive boilers, there is not much to see. I hope that the *Lelia* proves a more rewarding wreck.

The wreck of the confederate blockade runner *Lelia*.

The capsizing of the Liverpool Lifeboat on its way to rescue the crew of the *Lelia*.
She is being towed by the steam tug *Blazer*.

18

Chapter 4

Submarines

In the age of steam, the construction of a steam powered submarine was a challenge since burning coal consumes the oxygen in the air needed to breathe. The first successful vessel was built in Birkenhead from the design of a Liverpool inventor, the Reverend George Garrett. The *Resurgam* was tested in the docks and then she reached Rhyl from Liverpool under her own power and partly submerged. There was considerable naval interest in such a vessel and she was being taken by sea to Portsmouth to be demonstrated to the Navy when she was lost in Liverpool Bay. There was no loss of life.

Because she was lost while under tow, her precise location is unknown. Despite considerable efforts, the historic wreck has not been located. I give what guidance I can as to her probable whereabouts. She is a relatively small size and it could well be that her wreck is completely sanded in. A thorough search is nevertheless worth pursuing. It would be of great historical interest to recover her remains - she was the first powered submarine.

A very different submarine tragedy occurred just before the Second World War. The *Thetis* was undergoing acceptance trials in Liverpool Bay. She took water on board and ended up with her bow on the seabed with her stern clear of the surface. Only four of her crew managed to escape and the vessel was eventually beached on Anglesey. She was salvaged and refitted and renamed the *Thunderbolt* - so no wreckage exists in Liverpool Bay.

Resurgam

Submarine 30 tons displacement, 45 ft long, 9 ft beam.
Built: Cochrane & Co., Britannia Iron Works, Birkenhead 1879.
Engines: Steam Lamm engine, 1 boiler, 1 screw.
Date of wreck: 25 February 1880

Reverend George Garrett was very much the stereotype of a Victorian inventor and entrepreneur. He had full confidence in himself and his ideas. One of his innovations was a submarine. The main problem to be overcome was that of underwater propulsion, since steam power involved burning coal which used up the oxygen in the air. The Lamm engine relied on a store of compressed steam to give a limited underwater range - of 12 miles according to Garrett. The prototype was a small vessel with hardly room for her crew of three. Nevertheless she was the first manned submarine with engines. Her first sea trials took her as far as Rhyl. A delightful incident occurred en route when the intrepid submariners surfaced to get their bearings. They came up close to a sailing ship and asked directions. The Captain was amazed, more so when told they had been under his boat for some hours. The Captain pronounced 'Well, you are the three biggest fools I have ever met'.

At Rhyl she was overhauled and Garrett bought a steam yacht, the *Elfin*, to accompany her. The intention was to take the *Resurgam* to Portsmouth to demonstrate her to the Navy. The submarine and yacht left Rhyl at 10 pm on 24 February 1880. The weather got worse as they proceeded west. Off Great Ormes Head, the captain of the *Elfin* had to ask the crew of the *Resurgam* for help on the *Elfin*. A boat was sent to bring them aboard and George Price, the engineer from the *Resurgam*, went below to help mend the pumps. The *Elfin* took the *Resurgam* in tow. A gale developed which prevented the crew from returning to the *Resurgam*. They towed her through the night but since her conning tower hatch could not be closed from outside, she took water on board in the rough seas. This increased her weight and the next morning at 10 am the hawser parted. She then broke free and eventually sank.

The disaster did not end there. The *Elfin* took shelter in the Dee and anchored off Mostyn. The wind changed and her anchor chains broke. The *Elfin* was adrift and needed assistance. The *Iron King* came to the rescue but she rammed the *Elfin* making her a total loss. Nobody was killed in this sequence of nautical disasters. Garrett went to Liverpool to try and get help to look for the *Resurgam*, but the bad weather continued and no vessel was prepared to venture out.

The search for the wreck of the *Resurgam* has fascinated many people. One problem is that she was tiny - just 45 feet long and 30 tons. She was presumably heavily built, being a pressure vessel, but she could be easily engulfed in a shifting sandbank. The other problem is that it is not known exactly where she parted company with her escort and how long she drifted before sinking. She was lost at 10 am on Wednesday 25 February 1880 and high water was at 11.10 am that day. The tidal current would tend to take her west of her position when the tow parted. The *Elfin* had her in tow off Great Ormes Head and had lost her by the time she was herself wrecked on Salisbury Middle Bank in the Dee Estuary. This leaves a lot of sea.

The *Resurgam* at Birkenhead.

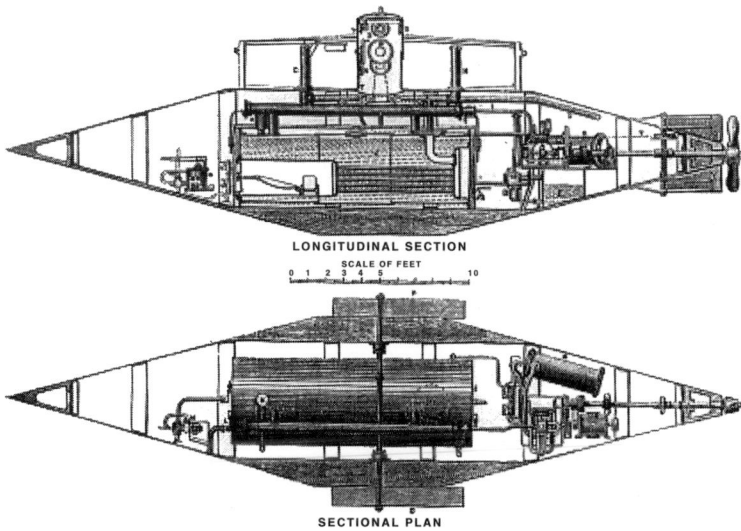

LONGITUDINAL SECTION

SCALE OF FEET

0 1 2 3 4 5   10

SECTIONAL PLAN

The plans of Garrett's submarine torpedo boat *Resurgam* built by Cochrane's in Birkenhead.

Thetis

Triton Class Submarine 1095 tons displacement, 240 ft long.
Built: Cammell Laird, Birkenhead 1939.
Date of wreck: 2 June 1939

In 1939 with the threat of war in Europe growing stronger, there was pressure to build up Britain's naval strength. In particular submarines were to be brought into service as fast as possible. The *Thetis* was the first of a new class of submarines which was being built by Cammell Laird at Birkenhead. She was ready for acceptance trials and it was decided to hold these nearby in Liverpool Bay. As well as her normal naval crew of about 50, she had Admiralty observers, shipyard personnel, 2 caterers and a Mersey pilot aboard. In total she carried 103 persons for her first diving trials in Liverpool Bay on 1 June 1939. These diving trials were expected to be very safe and uncomplicated. Perhaps for this reason, none of the extra persons accepted the invitation of her commander to disembark to her escorting surface vessel before diving commenced.

She was under the command of Lt.-Commander Bolus. The chief Admiralty observer was Captain Oram who was to oversee the tests. At 1.30 pm, when she was about 13 miles north of Llandudno, the crew prepared her for diving. Problems were apparent with her buoyancy. Even after using the auxiliary ballast tanks, she was light at the bow. The possibility of filling some of the forward torpedo tubes with water was then discussed. There were 6 torpedo tubes and tubes 5 and 6 were the lowest and opened under water even when the submarine was on the surface. There was some uncertainty as to whether these two tubes were empty or full of water when the *Thetis* was trimmed at Birkenhead. The forward part of the submarine was the responsibility of Lt. Frederick Woods. He was assigned to check on the state of these tubes.

Lt. Woods opened the test cocks on the rear doors of the torpedo tubes to see if there was water inside. No water came from the test cock of number 5 tube so he then opened the rear door of this tube to check for possible leaks. The tube was in fact full of water and, moreover, the bow cover was also open so that the tube was fully open to the sea. One of the main points raised in the inquiry was that Lt. Woods should have made sure that the bow cover was closed before opening the rear door to the torpedo tube. The test cock was subsequently found to have been blocked by paint - although a reamer was supplied to clear out the test cock should it be blocked.

On opening the rear door, a great pressure of water forced it open so it could not be shut again. Thinking that the torpedo tube itself must be fractured, Lt. Woods did not try to shut the bow cap, but ordered the front compartment to be isolated. Here again problems arose. The submarine was now sloping downward and the bulkhead door was hinged forward. It had to be pulled upwards to close it and this

The stern of the *Thetis* surrounded by rescue boats.

The *Thetis* at Cammell Laird's.

the men could not manage. Water was pouring in and the lights failed. Furniture was falling down on them. The men had to scramble back to close the next bulkhead door which they were able to secure safely. The front part of the submarine took on board a lot of water. Indeed the front two compartments became completely flooded. The weight of the water pushed her bow to the sea bed. Even by blowing the other ballast tanks she remained with her nose on the bottom. Running the engines in reverse did not help. She gradually settled to a more even keel - lying on the bottom at 40 metres below the surface and at a slope of only 6^0.

Captain Oram and Lt.-Commander Bolus conferred as to the best course of action. They released an indicator buoy and a smoke candle to alert the surface escort of their problem. Attempts were made to rid the front section of water. This involved sending in men wearing Davis breathing apparatus to try and close the rear door of torpedo tube 5. This was a very ambitious plan since two bulkheads had to be passed first and then the door closed and lever operated to hold it shut. The Davis breathing apparatus was designed for men ascending directly to the surface and was unsuited to manoeuvering in a confined space at 40 metres depth. The chance of succeeding and of returning alive was small. Nevertheless Lt. Woods and two volunteers tried but they could not stand the strain of the pressure.

The submarine had an escape hatch and carried Davis breathing apparatus sets. The escape procedure entailed entering a chamber which was first closed and then flooded. When the pressure was equalised, the top hatch to the outside could be raised and the men could pass through. The Davis equipment allowed them to breathe and gave them sufficient buoyancy to take them swiftly to the surface. Usually two men at a time entered the chamber. It was difficult for trained men to use under ideal conditions but in a dark, slippery, sloping submarine the procedure was frightening.

In any case, it was not sensible to use this means of escape until there was a sign that surface help was standing by. It was decided that senior officers should be the first to leave to help organise the rescue. The only other recourse of the trapped men was to pump out as much water and oil as possible to lighten the vessel so she might regain the surface. Gradually the pumping took effect until the stern remained bobbing above the waves with the whole vessel tilted at 40^0 to the horizontal since she was in water less deep than her length.

Her surface escort was a Liverpool tug *Grebecock* which carried a naval liaison officer, Lt. Coltart, and telegraphist. The primary function of the escort was to warn other vessels to keep clear of the submarine when it was submerged. The *Grebecock* was ordered to stand by half a mile off when the submarine was ready to dive. They saw the *Thetis* proceed to the west on the surface for a long time and then suddenly plunge below the surface at 2.58. Lt. Coltart did not realise immediately that anything was amiss. The tug tried to maintain station by steaming into the tide. When the *Thetis* did not reappear as planned, they sent a radio message to submarine command at Fort Blockhouse to ask the expected total time of the dive.

Receiving no answer, Lt. Coltart ordered the tug to anchor. She was in 40 metres and the anchor chain was of insufficient length. There was a delay of an hour while they roped two segments of chain together. It turned out subsequently that they were anchored about 4 miles WNW from the *Thetis*.

Alerted by Fort Blockhouse, the destroyer HMS *Brazen* arrived at 9 pm and commenced a search for the missing submarine. Since the *Grebecock* was out of position, the search to the west of her position was not successful. Further confusion came from several aircraft reports of buoys which proved to be irrelevant. Even though the *Thetis* sent up indicator lights from time to time, these were not spotted. At 3.15 am in the night the MDHB salvage vessel *Vigilant* joined the search.

Finally at 7.50 am on the morning of 2 June, the *Brazen* searched east of the *Grebecock* and sighted the stern of the *Thetis* protruding 6 metres from the surface. This remarkable result had been achieved by the steady pumping of the Cammell Laird workers aboard. The air quality aboard was deteriorating. When the sound signal from the *Brazen* was heard, Captain Oram and Lt. Woods used the escape hatch to reach the surface to help organise the rescue. At this time the escape hatch was not particularly far underwater and the surface rescuers expected that many would be able to escape. An experiment was then made to send up four men together but all four were drowned. It took some effort in the dark, sloping, slippery conditions to remove the bodies. Only two more men successfully used the escape hatch: stoker Arnold and engine fitter Shaw surfaced at 10 am. They confirmed that the remaining men on board were suffering from the build up of carbon dioxide in the air.

The MDHB salvage vessel *Vigilant* joined in the rescue attempt and passed a wire hawser under the stern of the *Thetis*. Strenuous attempts were made to cut a hole in her stern to let men out but this proved too difficult from a small boat bobbing close by. The submarine weighed over 1000 tons and was too heavy to be lifted off the seabed. The rising tide caused the wire hawser to break at 3.10 pm. The submarine sank from view with the remaining men still inside. She was visited by a diver during the night who reported that he thought he heard faint tapping. A later dive did not confirm this and the rescue operation became a salvage operation.

A whole saga of poor decisions and small mistakes compounded to make this great tragedy. The vessel had too many people on board. Her trim was not satisfactory so that adjustments had to be made at sea. The test cock that could show that there was indeed water in number 5 torpedo tube was blocked by bituminous paint and a reamer provided to clear out any blockage in the test cock was not used. The bow cover controls for all 6 torpedo tubes were set to neutral instead of closed. There was negligence in opening the rear door of the torpedo tube without checking that the bow cover indicators showed closed. When water rushed in through the rear door, the bow cover was not closed to stem the flow. Then there was failure to close satisfactorily the first bulkhead door so that two compartments became flooded. The arrangements for communicating with the surface escort were inadequate. The alarm was raised belatedly by the surface escort. The surface escort lost contact with the submarine and drifted off station because she had inadequate anchor chains. Help from salvage vessels was requested only later on in the rescue. An attempt to cut a hole in the stern was left until too late.

Many men must have felt partly to blame and it must have been agonising to realise that though the rescue boats were just feet away, their help would be insufficient to save the men inside the stricken vessel. For the crew inside, after having their hopes raised by sound signals from the rescue party, the tragic end does not bear thinking about.

Because of her great weight, the vessel could not be lifted directly. Indeed she was eventually lifted by attaching slings to barges at low tide, towing the barges closer to shore as the tide rose, and then shortening the slings at the next low tide. In this way she was raised a few metres at a time and brought to Traeth Bychan beach on the west coast of Anglesey 5 months later. Her dead were taken to Holyhead for burial. The submarine was returned to Cammell Laird's and was refitted as HMS *Thunderbolt*. She sank two German submarines and five supply ships before being destroyed by depth charges off Sicily in 1943 with the loss of 62 men.

Chapter 5

Irish sea ferries

In previous centuries, the ferry service to Ireland had used the Dee ports for embarkation. With the silting up of the Dee estuary and the coming of the railway, Liverpool took over the role of natural ferry port for Ireland. Liverpool has long been closely linked to the Isle of Man. Passenger services were also run along the North Wales Coast. Disasters involving passenger ferries give rise to strong emotions. Despite the large number of ferry services, there has been a good safety record, with few serious losses in Liverpool Bay.

The largest loss of life occurred when the Isle of Man ferry *Ellan Vannin* was overwhelmed by rough seas at the entrance to the Liverpool shipping channel. She had the reputation of being a sound and sturdy ship, but the conditions were atrocious when she neared Liverpool Bar. Her plight is rather well known since it was publicised by the song performed by the Spinners folk group.

In contrast, the earliest such wreck is a bit of a mystery. Divers recovered the bell of the *Dublin* from a wreck. In the 1880's, this vessel operated a regular Liverpool - Dublin service with cargo and passengers for the Tedcastle Line. After much research, I have been able to find brief reports of her demise. One almost gets the feeling that the Tedcastle Line wished to keep her loss unadvertised so as not to deter trade.

The largest ferry to be lost was the incoming Belfast ferry *Munster* which was sunk by a magnetic mine in 1940. She was a relatively new ship and was flying the Irish tricolour to proclaim her neutrality. Of course the mine was no respecter of flags! In this case there was thankfully no loss of life but much drama. The *Munster* is also one of the wrecks often visited by divers and anglers and the present state of the wreck is described.

Dublin

Irish steamship 599 tons gross, 176 ft long, 28 ft beam, 14 ft draught.
Built: Walpole and Webb, Dublin 1866.
Engines: Compound steam engines, 90 hp, installed 1882 by V. Coates & Co. (Lim)
Belfast.
Owners: R. Tedcastle, registered Dublin.
Date of wreck: 26 October 1888
Location: 53^0 29.60' N 3^0 38.00' W
Distance from New Brighton: 21 nautical miles.
Depth at low water: 31m seabed, 33m scour, 26m to top of wreck.

Robert Tedcastle was a Scot from Dumfrieshire who set up a shipping business
based at Dublin. Initially his ships were mainly involved in bringing coal to Dublin.
His first steamer was the *Dublin*. She was an iron screw steamer with three masts,
machinery aft and a well deck. The Company was one of the first to use steamers
to carry passengers on the Liverpool-Dublin route in 1872. During the 1880's, they
had 3 steamers (*Dublin, Magnet* and *Adela*) providing a regular Liverpool - Dublin
service. The Tedcastle steamers had a black funnel with 2 white bands. Their ships
were primarily cargo vessels and coal was usually carried to Ireland and cattle
were often carried as return cargo. The City of Dublin Steam Packet Company also
ran a Liverpool - Dublin service and their boats were paddle steamers intended
for passenger service. In order to compete with the higher standard of passenger
amenities on the City of Dublin steamers, Tedcastle's set lower fares. Deck (or
steerage) passengers paid a single fare of 3 shillings while cabin passengers paid
8 shillings compared to the fares of 5 shillings and 13 shillings on the City of
Dublin boats. The services of a steward and stewardess were provided for cabin
passengers on the Tedcastle ships. Robert Tedcastle and Co. became Tedcastle and
McCormick and were eventually taken over by the B and I line in 1919.

The fate of the *Dublin* would have gone unnoticed if it were not for her discovery by
divers. The presence of wreckage on the sea bed was well known but the identity
of the ship was a mystery. Her secret was revealed by the name found inscribed
on her bell by divers. The boss of her steering wheel has also been recovered with
her name on it.

There is a brief report in the Board of Trade Casualty Return for 1888 which indicates
that the *Dublin* was lost as a result of a collision with the *Longford* in a position
approximately 4 miles west of the North West Lightship. The local newspapers of
the time give very little prominence to this collision and it appears that the ships'
owners were anxious to play down the incident. Indeed Tedcastle's advertisement
for their service continues to mention the *Dublin* until the end of 1888.

The *Longford* was a paddle steamer of 817 tons gross belonging to the rival City of
Dublin Steam Packet Company. She was bound for Liverpool from Dublin with

The steamer *Gipsy* lying with her back broken in Avon Gorge. She was a similar vessel engaged in similar trade between Ireland and England to the *Dublin*.

The *Ellan Vannin*.

cattle, general cargo and passengers under the command of Captain Penstone. The *Dublin* had left Garston bound for Dublin with coal, general cargo and several passengers. Captain Staney took the *Dublin* into the Mersey on Friday 26 October around high water which was at 2am. By 5am she was off the North Wales coast when she was struck amidships by the bows of the *Longford*. The *Dublin* was the smaller vessel and she was damaged in a more vulnerable place. She foundered almost immediately. The crew of the *Dublin* were fortunately able to get off in time. Those in their bunks had to turn out half clothed and the rest of the crew had to rush to get the boats ready so they left in what they stood up in. Fortunately there was no injury to life or limb. The crew in the boats were towed by the *Longford* to Liverpool. There was great excitement when the *Longford* arrived at the Liverpool Landing Stage since she had her bows stoved in underwater and a sail draped around them to help seal the leak.

I have been unable to find a photograph of the *Dublin*. Instead the *Gipsy* is shown since she was a similar vessel engaged in a similar trade and had been built at Waterford in Ireland in 1857.

The *Dublin* lies quite close to the wreck of the coaster *Penstone* on the sea bed. They were both lost as a result of collision. The Hydrographic Office thought at one time that this site might be the wreck of the *Albanian*, a Bibby cargo steamer that sank in 1877. The *Albanian* is now known to lie further west. The *Dublin* is a much older and larger vessel than the *Penstone* and it is a very rewarding dive site. The wreck is upright and fairly intact, except for the bow section. The counter stern has rudder and single propeller. The bow lies south east and the stern north west.

Ellan Vannin

Passenger steamship 380 tons gross, 199 ft long, 22 ft beam, 11 ft draught.
Built: Tod and McGregor, Glasgow 1860, conversion work Barrow 1883.
Engines: 3 cylinder compound steam engines, 100rhp, twin screw, built Westray, Copeland at Barrow 1883.
Owners: Isle of Man Steam Packet Company, registered Douglas.
Date of wreck: 3 December 1909
Location: 53^0 32.02' N 3^0 16.90' W
Distance from New Brighton: 11 nautical miles.
Depth at low water: 11m seabed.

The *Ellan Vannin* started life as the *Mona's Isle* - an iron paddle steamer linking the Isle of Man to the mainland. She was converted in 1883 to twin screw propulsion with new engines and renamed. Her new name was the Manx for 'Isle of Man' - Mona's Isle. She could carry up to 300 passengers with a crew of 14. She had cabin accommodation for about 50 passengers. Later in her career, however, she was reserved for the routes with less traffic since she was relatively small compared to the other ships in the Isle of Man Steam Packet fleet. She mainly sailed from Ramsey at the North of the Isle of Man to Whitehaven, Liverpool and to Scottish ports. Though a relatively small ship she had a reputation as being tough. To fulfil the daily mail contract she had often threaded her way to sea through many vessels sheltering at Ramsey from a storm.

On December 3, she left Ramsey at 1.13 am bound for Liverpool with 15 passengers, a crew of 21, mail and 60 tons of cargo (sheep, pigs and vegetables). The weather was moderate when she set sail and her master, Captain James Teare of Douglas, had 18 years of experience of the run and did not expect unusually bad weather even though the barometer was falling. During the passage the wind built up to a severe North West gale - force 11. At 6.35 am in the morning she arrived at Liverpool Bar with tremendous seas running. The storm was one of the worst ever experienced with waves estimated as 7 metres high. She foundered between the Bar and the Q1 buoy with the loss of all passengers and crew. It appears that she must have broached on being swept before the seas. She filled and sank by the stern. She was battered by the huge waves which caused further damage to her bows.

Her position could located because her masts were breaking the surface. She was inspected by divers who reported damage to the bow area and that the lifeboat davits had been turned out ready for lowering. The subsequent Board of Trade inquiry rejected the possibility of collision as a cause of the loss and decided that the cause was extreme weather conditions with no blame attached to the master, crew or Company.

This story was read by Hugh Jones of the Spinners folk group and he wrote a song about the tragedy of the *Ellan Vannin*. This became well known after being performed on BBC TV in the summer of 1976.

The charted position of the wreck of the *Ellan Vannin* is given above. The wreckage was dispersed using explosives by the MDHB soon after she sank so as not to be an obstruction to shipping. I have searched in this area with magnetometer and found a weak signal indicating the presence of ferrous metal. I have not obtained any echo sounder signal coming from any material above the sea bed. However, the Kingfisher chart shows one 'fastener' nearby so presumably some parts of the wreck still stand proud of the sea bed. The visibility underwater is poor but diving is feasible since the location is quite shallow which should enable any wreckage to be seen. It is possible she is now completely covered in sand and silt but I shall be very interested to hear from any diver who finds wreckage.

Munster

Passenger motor ship 4302 tons gross, 353 ft long, 50 ft beam, 14 ft draught.
Built: 1938 Harland and Wolff, Belfast.
Engines: 20 cylinder oil engines, 1347 nhp, 2 screws.
Owners: Coast Lines, registered Dublin.
Date of wreck: 7 Feb 1940
Location: 53^0 35.96' N 3^0 26.75' W
Distance from New Brighton: 17 miles.
Depth at low water: 23m seabed, 24m scour, 18m to top of wreck.

The *Munster* and her sister ship the *Leinster* were new vessels built in 1937/8 for the Dublin - Liverpool service. A strike in Dublin prevented the completion of staging needed to berth them, so they began their career on the Belfast - Liverpool run. Prior to the war, Irish registered vessels had worn the Red Ensign. After the outbreak of war, they flew the tricolour of the Irish Free State. This lead to a dispute because the crews objected to sailing neutral ships through English waters in wartime without danger money. The strike by the crew resulted in both ships being laid up at Barrow. After a suitable agreement was reached, the *Munster* left Barrow on 11 December 1939 on charter to the Belfast Steamship Company. Her hull was painted black with the Irish Tricolour on each side. This precaution was not to save her from loss.

The *Munster* was fitted with many of the latest refinements. She was designed for night crossings so was appointed with staterooms, cabins and berths for passengers. She had high quality fittings in the passenger dining rooms and lounges; red leather door coverings, marble fireplaces and oriental vases, for example. She was the first ship to offer ship-to-shore radio telephone as a service for passengers and the first with fluorescent electric lighting of the passenger accommodation. She also had three cargo holds with electric winches at each hatch. She was a twin screw vessel with diesel engines giving 19 knots. She had accommodation for 1500 passengers and contemporary photographs show her with a huge number of portholes. She was the largest cross channel motor ship in the world.

On Tuesday 8 February 1940, the *Munster* sailed from Belfast with 180 passengers on board. Her listed cargo included thread, eggs, animal gut, textiles and poultry. Since the sinking of the *El Oso* by a mine in Liverpool Bay a few weeks earlier, she would have followed the swept channel as far as possible. By 6 am the next morning, she was close to Liverpool Bar. A magnetic mine caused an enormous explosion. The lights went out, the fore part of the vessel was lifted out of the water and there was damage on the bridge, particularly the port side. The radio equipment was destroyed so she could not transmit a distress call. Most people were asleep but they quickly went to boat stations. She carried 7 large lifeboats and a motor boat. The injured were sought out and lowered first to the boats.

The Belfast - Liverpool ferry *Munster.*

There was no panic, although contemporary reports tell of some passengers being 'scantily clad'. Everyone on board was able to take to the boats. A baby in arms slept through the whole episode.

Captain Paisley, though injured with a broken arm, was reluctant to leave the ship and the chief officer, Mr. Wrigley, had to persuade him. The *Munster* was listing to port and down by the head and she was reported as sinking in about $1\frac{1}{2}$ hours. She was not quite 2 years old.

Some lifeboats became waterlogged but the ship's motor lifeboat was able to pick up people. Flares from the *Munster* had been seen by a small coasting vessel, the *Ringwall*. She picked up the survivors from the boats after about 3 hours. By this time some of the lifeboats had taken in a lot of water and were close to submerging. There was a running sea and the lifeboats drifted from the ship's side so were towed alongside by the motor lifeboat. Everyone was saved and only 20 injuries were reported. A young Belfast doctor, Dr. Gallagher, was aboard and he was highly praised for the way he tended to the injured. The passengers and crew were landed at Liverpool.

The Admiralty war loss record quotes the mine explosion as occurring at 53^0 36' N 3^0 24' W. The position quoted above is that given by MDHB and by the Hydrographic Office although they describe the site as 'presumed *Munster*'. The position charted has changed a little in recent years and I give the corrected position. This agrees with my own position determination.

This wreck site is an excellent dive with more of a scrapyard than an identifiable ship to see. There is an extensive area of tangled wreckage, some portholes, and two small cylindrical objects some 4 metres long. I first dived it in 1985 and the wreckage appeared not to have been dived before that. I remember that there were large lobsters walking around everywhere - and one of them was sitting in an intact loose porthole. Such is the stuff of diver's dreams! Some large portholes have been found on this site. This wreck always has a good variety of fish life, particularly large pollack and ling - and it is still home to more than its fair share of lobsters. I have even seen a fisherman catch a lobster with rod and line. The area and amount of wreckage is much less than one would expect from a ship as big as the *Munster*. However, the *Munster* is recorded as being cleared by the Admiralty Wreck Disposal Vessel HMS *Annet* in 1947. Presumably most of her wreckage lies under the sea bed in the trench created by explosive charges in the clearance. The part of the wreck above the sand seems to be from the forward superstructure. The force of these explosions would explain why only tangled wreckage survives to be seen today.

Chapter 6

Wartime Convoy Losses

After the experience gained painfully in the First World War, the convoy system for merchant shipping was put into operation from the beginning of the Second World War. Liverpool was the destination for many of the trans-atlantic convoys. From the viewpoint of Liverpool, this meant groups of up to 70 vessels arriving together and having to be assigned berths. Even within sight of Liverpool, the danger was not passed. Early in the war magnetic mines were laid in the approaches to Liverpool. These were triggered by the slight change in the natural magnetic field caused by a steel vessel passing close by. Even though the Royal Navy had experimented with magnetic mines before the war, they were not equipped to deal with them. Luckily, a German seaplane dropped two magnetic mines on mudflats in the Thames Estuary. They were located and defused by a mine disposal team who thus learnt their secrets. This lead to the development of an efficient minesweeping method and to the 'degaussing' of ship's hulls. This 'degaussing' worked by passing an electrical current through cables around the ship's hull which cancelled out the ship's own magnetism - so making it safe from magnetic mines. These measures took some time to come into full operation and during the winter of 1939/40, there were many losses caused by magnetic mines.

The first such loss on the West Coast was the *El Oso* on 11 January 1940. She was sunk by a mine laid by submarine *U-30* a few days earlier. The *El Oso* was an oil tanker returning fully laden from Peru and it was very lucky that the majority of the crew escaped unharmed. The following weeks saw the *Cairnross, Munster, Chagres* and *Counsellor* similarly lost to magnetic mines in Liverpool Bay. After this series of disasters, the losses decreased as minesweeping became more efficient.

As well as rescuing the crew, the authorities had to keep the shipping lanes open. Thus any wrecks near the shipping lane (such as the tanker *Dosinia*) were marked by wreck buoys. The MDHB were able to use explosives to reduce the underwater obstruction caused by a wreck. However, for larger wrecks, the quantity of explosives needed was greater than they were allowed to use. Thus the Admiralty were contracted to provide the clearance. Indeed they had several Wreck Disposal

Vessels busy around Britain until 1950. The method was to place a series of charges on one side of the hull. This then created a trench in the sea bed into which the wreckage moved. In the case of the *Dosinia*, 666 depth charges were reported to have been used in total.

Many wartime casualties were salvaged by the MDHB using their salvage vessel *Vigilant*, tugs and other vessels. As well as complete salvage, some wrecks may have been towed from the position of the mine explosion to take them further from the channel. This may explain why several wrecks are charted as several miles from the recorded position of the mining.

In the early months of the War, the newspapers carried details of the losses and of the heroism of individual seamen. Later, the censor struck out all bad news and only a total of tonnage lost was published. In some cases, I have been able to get first hand accounts from crew who were on these vessels when they were mined. Thus a clearer picture is now available of the drama of these losses. In some cases a supplementary picture comes from the present state of the wreck as revealed by diving.

Later in the war, the mine menace was under control. The *Stanleigh* was sunk by aircraft. Her wreck has not been definitely located. Another wartime loss was the Greek vessel *Nestos*. She ran aground on the Hoyle Bank. The reduction in sea marks during wartime contributed to this navigational error. Her wreckage is still very prominent at low tide.

El Oso

Steam tanker 7267 tons gross, 440 ft long, 57 ft beam, 34 ft draught.
Built: 1921 Armstrong Whitworth, Newcastle.
Engines: steam triple compound, 678 nhp.
Owners: Lobitos Oilfields (managed Bowrings), registered London.
Date of wreck: 11 Jan 1940.
Location: $53^0 37.43'$ N $3^0 23.42'$ W
Distance from New Brighton: 17 nautical miles.
Depth at low water: 30m seabed, 32m scour, 17m to top of wreck.

The *El Oso* was a British registered and built tanker which was mined. She was the first casualty on the West Coast and there was much publicity at the time - even though the censor insisted on 'a north west port' rather than 'Liverpool'. Most of the crew of 36 were from Merseyside. I have been able to get first hand reports from some of those who sailed in her on this fateful trip: Captain F. H. Simpson, the third mate Mr. Hoffmann and the ship's carpenter Mr. Harry Shakeshaft. Mr. Shakeshaft was one of many who had volunteered as soon as war was declared and were on

The oil tanker *El Oso*.

The *El Oso* after the mine explosion.

their first Merchant Marine posting when she left Liverpool in October 1939 bound for Peru.

The *El Oso* took on board a cargo of 9238 tons of Peruvian crude oil and 511 tons of casinghead gas from Lobitos oilfield. Her route to Ellesmere Port took her through the Panama canal and then across the Atlantic from Halifax in convoy with about 72 other ships. She had left Halifax on Boxing day and arrived off Liverpool on January 11. She was waiting in choppy seas to pick up a pilot after the convoy dispersed. She was 6 miles west of the Bar Light and it was 9 am. A magnetic mine was triggered by her massive iron content and exploded amidships.

The casinghead gas in her side tanks was like liquid petroleum gas and was kept under pressure. With such a volatile cargo, it is amazing that she did not explode when mined. Crude oil squirted everywhere covering many of the crew. Again there was no fire, although the sound of escaping steam must have been worrying. Many of those injured were off watch in the forward part of the ship when the anchor chain was thrown around by the force of the explosion. The flying bridge amidships was wrecked and many of the crew suffered from shock.

One can understand the urgency with which Captain Simpson ordered the crew to abandon ship. Some of the boats were damaged in the explosion and while one boat was being lowered, the ship lurched and those handling the ropes were thrown across the deck causing the boat to drop to the water end up. One boat cast off quickly to pick up a man who had fallen from the ladder. This boat took about 6 crew with the third mate. A second boat was also lowered, Captain Simpson and the majority of the crew got into her from the poop deck down lifelines - some skinning their hands in getting down.

Three of the crew were lost - two able seamen (A. Douglas of Birkenhead and A. E. Robinson of Liverpool) and the second cook (M. Lynch of Ormskirk). Eight were listed as badly injured, one of whom (E. P. Bryant) subsequently died in hospital. Some of the losses came from those who were in the sea which was covered with a thick layer of crude oil. They may have been overcome by fumes or choked when trying to swim in the oil covered sea.

The survivors in the boats rowed as quickly as they could to get away from the ship in case of fire or further explosion. The officers rowed too and the chief engineer rowed with one hand since his other hand was injured. They were picked up by a destroyer HMS *Walker* from the convoy escort. Nets were put over the side and after the fit men had got aboard, the injured were gathered up. There was some delay in picking up the men from one of the boats while the escorts looked for possible U-boats.

The wreck now lies some 3 miles north of the Bar Light so presumably she drifted afloat for some time - kept from sinking by the oil in her tanks which is lighter than water. Indeed the illustration from a contemporary newspaper shows her lying with her back broken and steam billowing from her stern but in no immediate danger of sinking. She was an obstruction to shipping, so a buoy was placed nearby. Oil seeped out of the wreck for many years although it has stopped now. She was surveyed in 1980 with the possibility of reducing her further by explosives. No such action has been taken so she is still relatively ship-shape in parts.

The *El Oso* is the largest deep-water wreck and the easiest to find. A north cardinal buoy named 'El Oso' is 0.1 nautical mile north of the wreck. The wreck is 200 metres long with prominent scour trenches. It is in two parts with the stern to the north lying on its port side and the bows to the south lying upside down. There are some overhanging sections of wreckage so the wreck can be dangerous for the inexperienced. Visibility under water is best in the summer and autumn. The wreck has been partly reduced by explosives but big sections are still visible - particularly around the stern. There is a deep scour around the west side of the stern section.

Cairnross

Steamship 5494 tons gross, 425 ft long, 55 ft beam, 26 ft draught.
Built: Doxford, Sunderland 1921.
Engines: three steam turbines (3 single-ended boilers) built Parsons Marine Steam Turbines, Newcastle, 1 screw.
Owners: Cairn Line, registered Newcastle.
Date of wreck: 17 Jan 1940
Location: 53^0 30.90' N 3^0 33.10' W
Distance from New Brighton: 19 nautical miles.
Depth at low water: 30m seabed, 30m scour, 26m to top of wreck.

The *Cairnross* was the first British cargo ship to have turbine engines. She was carrying a cargo of coal plus some 50 tons of general cargo including earthenware. Her destination was St. Johns in Canada. She was leaving Liverpool when mined by enemy action 6.5 miles 276^0 from the Bar Light Vessel at 5.20 pm. The explosion flung the crew from their bunks and water flooded the stokehold. In the stokehold it was dark and there were clouds of steam. The ladder was broken so it was difficult to find a way out. One fireman injured his head trying to find the way up and was helped by the others. The crew went to their stations without panic and the boats were launched. All 48 men were able to escape in two lifeboats. The ship sank within an hour of setting the mine off. The crew were picked up from the boats by a destroyer from the convoy after about 3 hours. Perhaps the *Cairnross* was unlucky - being the thirteenth in the convoy. Yet no lives were lost.

Although this is one of the larger ships wrecked in Liverpool bay, the area of prominent wreckage appears quite small - consisting mainly of her boilers. There is scattered wreckage over a large area, however. Parts are rather sanded in. Indeed, there are some impressive sand waves nearby - so make quite sure of the location and echo sounder signals before diving.

Chagres

Steamship 5406 tons gross, 400 ft long, 51 ft beam, 30 ft draught.
Built: Stephen and Sons, Glasgow 1927.
Engines: Steam triple compound of 447 nhp, built A. Stephen at Glasgow.
Owners: Elders and Fyffes, registered Glasgow.
Date of wreck: 9 Feb 1940
Location: 53^0 34.92' N 3^0 41.40' W
Distance from New Brighton: 25 nautical miles.
Depth at low water: 36m seabed, 40m scour, 28m to top of wreck.

The *Chagres*, despite her foreign sounding name, was a British cargo steamship. She was on a voyage from Victoria (Nigeria) to Garston with a cargo of 1500 tons of bananas. During the early hours of the morning of 10 February, she was sunk by a mine in a position reported as 5.5 miles west of the Bar Light Vessel. Of her crew of 62, two were lost and 7 were injured sufficiently to need treatment in hospital. Her master was Captain Hugh Roberts who had been decorated in the first World War for shaking off a U-boat. The explosion blew out steam pipes and scalded several men. The lights failed and one fireman was trapped below by fallen metal and could not be pulled out. By the time a light could be found so that help could be sent below, the ship was sinking fast and there was no time to go back. The other loss was of the bosun who was within two feet of being saved by his mates who pushed an oar to him in the water. He was too exhausted to hold on.

Because she is relatively deep and further from shore than most of the wrecks described, the under water visibility can be very good. I have experienced 20 metre visibility. She lies north west to south east. She is reasonably upright and fairly intact with her stern south. A mast sticks up prominently amidships - indeed some anglers reported to me that her funnel was identified by their sonar! The engine components are very clearly visible and some of the collapsed bridge is evident. This wreck is excellent for marine life and it is a popular target for wreck fishermen.

The *Cairnross*.

The *Chagres*.

Counsellor

Steamship 5068 tons gross, 395 ft long, 52 ft beam, 28 ft draught.
Built: Connell, Glasgow 1926.
Engines: Steam triple compound of 464 nhp (2 double-ended boilers), built Rowan & Co., Glasgow.
Owners: Charente (managed Harrisons), registered Liverpool.
Date of wreck: 8 March 1940
Location: 53^0 37.77' N 3^0 21.83' W.
Distance from New Brighton: 17 nautical miles.
Depth at low water: 25m seabed, 26m scour, 22m to top of wreck.

The Harrison line had its origins in coasters trading in the Liverpool region and then expanded by importing brandy from France. This is the origin of the name Charente. By 1920, they had 54 steamships trading worldwide with names taken from professions. They lost 31 ships in the second World War and the *Counsellor* was one of the first.

She was bound from New Orleans via Halifax to Liverpool with a general cargo including cotton. She set off a magnetic mine at 10 am at a position given as 6 miles west of the Bar Light Vessel. She began to settle immediately and the crew of 68 gathered on deck and lowered the boats. There was no panic and it was like boat drill. They rowed for 45 minutes before being picked up by a warship from the convoy. As one survivor reported: they got safely on board without wetting their feet. One or two crew had superficial injuries and one man broke a leg getting into the lifeboats. Her master was Captain H. Coates of Crosby.

The position given for the mine explosion is west of the Bar Light Vessel and the wreck is charted as north of it. She must have drifted (or been towed) some distance before sinking. This is feasible since the picture of her after the mine explosion does not show her in immediate danger of sinking.

This wreck lies quite close to the *El Oso* - about 1 nautical mile at 070^0 from the buoy. It is much more sanded in with only some parts lying more than a metre or so above the seabed. It is less dived and has brass fittings and portholes lying around.

The Harrison cargo liner *Counsellor*.

The *Counsellor* abandoned in Liverpool Bay after **being damaged by a mine**.

Dosinia

Motor tanker 8053 tons gross, 465 ft long, 59 ft beam, 33 ft draught.
Built: Lithgows, Glasgow 1938
Engines: 8 cylinder oil engines, 503 nhp, built J. G. Kincard, Gourock.
Owners: Anglo Saxon Petroleum Company, registered London.
Date of wreck: 26 October 1940
Location: (stern) 53^0 31.74' N 3^0 16.97' W
Location: (bows) 53^0 31.73' N 3^0 16.15' W
Distance from New Brighton: 12 nautical miles.
Depth at low water: 12m seabed, 11m to top of wreck.

The *Dosinia* was an oil tanker used to carry petroleum. She had her machinery aft and a cruiser stern. She left Stanlow on the Mersey for Table Bay, Cape Town in ballast. She was mined near the Q1 buoy at 5.30 pm on 26 October 1940. About the same time, another outward bound ship, the Belgian steamer *Katanga*, was also mined but she managed to limp back to Liverpool. The mine exploded near the engine room of the *Dosinia*, blowing part of the stern away. Her hull was extensively damaged near the engine room. The pilot vessel *Walter J. Chambers* under the command of Captain Leitch was about a half mile away. Rather than pick up survivors by ship's boats, he decided to bring his larger vessel alongside the stricken *Dosinia* which would be a speedier way of getting the injured aboard before the *Dosinia* sank. The pilots and apprentice pilots boarded the *Dosinia* and assisted the injured. When all the crew of 56 were apparently accounted for, Captain Leitch was just about to cast off when sounds of moaning were heard coming from the engine room. Pilots Clarke and Snowball went aboard to investigate and found a badly injured man lying across some pipes. They were able to get him up on deck and then onto the pilot boat before the *Dosinia* sank. The fireman who had been brought off had a fractured thigh and pelvis and badly injured head. Captain Leitch and Pilots Clarke and Snowball were presented with medals for bravery by the Liverpool Shipwreck and Humane Society.

The *Dosinia* broke in two and the stern grounded listing to starboard. The forward portion sank further east. The two parts are charted as separate wrecks. She lies in the mouth of the main Formby shipping channel and has been reduced by explosives by the Admiralty under contract with the MDHB. It was a major undertaking to push an 8000 ton ship under the sea bed. The clearance was completed in 1950 by HMS *Fetlar*. She reported reducing the stern section to 10 metres below MLWS in an area where the sea bed was 12.5 metres deep. Today, the charted position of the stern section gives a large magnetometer reading confirming the presence of substantial ferrous material. I have not been able to find any sign of wreckage on the echo sounder, but the Kingfisher chart shows 'fasteners' nearby so some parts of the wreck lie above the seabed where they have snagged fishing nets. The position of the *Dosinia* is close to that of the *Ellan Vannin*.

The *Dosinia*.

The *Stanleigh*.

Stanleigh

Steamship 1802 tons gross, 260 ft long, 38 ft beam, 17 ft draught.
Built: G. Seebeck, Wesermunde, Germany 1912.
Engines: triple compound steam engines, two boilers, 186 nhp, built G. Seebeck.
Owners: Stanhope Steamship Co. (managed J. A. Billmeir), registered London.
Date of wreck: 14 March 1941
Reported Location: 12 miles 288^0 from Bar Light Vessel

The *Stanleigh* had started life as the *Ernst Hugo Stinnes* after her construction in Germany just before the first World War. Successively renamed the *Corpath* then *Prekla*, she acquired her final name in 1937 when she joined the fleet of British merchant entrepreneur Jack Billmeir. After many unsuccessful ventures in shipping, he finally found his way to fortune by supplying the Republican side during the Spanish Civil War. He bought old vessels, since the loss insurance was less, and used them to import sorely needed material into North West Spain. Many were attacked by General Franco's Nationalist forces. The *Stanleigh* was herself hit by a bomb while lying at Valencia on 28 July 1938. This bomb caused a fire and injured two crewmen. The fire was brought under control quickly. She was attacked again at Valencia on 5 August when two bombs landed alongside her. Her superstructure was damaged but not seriously and she was quickly put back in service.

The *Stanleigh* was nearly 30 years old by then but she had been fitted with large topside tanks and still had a role to play. She was a steamer with her machinery aft - looking like a large coaster. She had two single-ended boilers with 4 corrugated furnaces with a grate surface of 5 square metres. She was used to transport material around the coast of Britain during the Second World War.

Although she survived enemy actions in Spain, she was to be less lucky next time she was hit by a bomb. On a voyage from Devonport to Barrow in ballast on His Majesty's Service, she had a crew of 22 and one gunner aboard. She was in convoy in the Irish Sea under the command of Captain Bibbings when she was attacked by a German aircraft. A bomb hit her and she started to sink. There were 6 survivors but 17 men, including Captain Bibbings, were killed.

Her listed position when bombed is close to the position of the *Chagres*. Several other wrecks are charted in locations quite distant from their reported position when attacked. Thus one possibility is that the charted wreck 'Unknown A' is the *Stanleigh*. This is discussed further in the section on Miscellaneous Wrecks.

Nestos

Greek steamship 5764 tons gross, 405 ft long, 52 ft beam, 32 ft draught.
Built: W. Pickergill and Sons, Sunderland 1919.
Engines: Steam triple compound (3 boilers) of 447 nhp, built Richardsons at Sunderland.
Owners: Theofano Maritime, Chios, Greece (managed N. G. Livanos).
Date of wreck: 2 April 1941
Location: 53^0 24.78' N 3^0 14.35' W.
Distance from New Brighton: 8 nautical miles.
Depth at low water: dries 5.4 metres.

The *Nestos* started life as the *Arabian Prince* owned by Prince Lines (Furness Withy and Co.) and registered in Newcastle. Her first year of service as the *Arabian Prince* was a year of disaster. Her propeller shaft fractured in mid-Atlantic, there was a fire in the hold in Gibraltar and then she was caught in a hurricane at Port Louis on Mauritius. She was later renamed the *Zenada* and owned by the Z Steamship Co., managed by Turner Brightman of London. In 1933 she passed into Greek ownership, managed by N. G. Livanos.

In 1941 she met more bad luck - ending up stranded on the Hoyle bank. The reason for this has been hard to discover. As it happens there was an English mate aboard: Mr. White. He had survived the torpedoing of his ship the *Anglo-Peruvian* on an outward convoy. He ended up in Halifax and joined the *Nestos* to get back across the Atlantic. His report explains what happened.

Carrying a cargo of 7750 tons of sulphur from New Orleans to Garston, the *Nestos* was ordered to join an eastbound convoy in Halifax to gain protection crossing the Atlantic en route to Liverpool. The weather was very rough and after breakdowns she became separated from her convoy. Eventually she fell in with a convoy coming from the south. By the morning of the 33rd day out from Halifax, in thick fog, the *Nestos* was alone again. A bearing was taken early in the morning on land presumed to be Point Lynas on Anglesey. Keeping course for Liverpool Bar, at dead slow speed, she ran aground at 12.30. They radioed for assistance but it was not in the correct code so the message was ignored because it might have come from a German U-boat. The sea was calm and Captain Pandelis Tsiropinos ordered the crew to try to pull themselves off the sandbank by running out the anchors, but with no success. The next morning the fog lifted and they saw that they were on the West Hoyle bank just north of Hilbre Island. At about the same time a pilot boat came alongside to give assistance. Their position was outside the area swept of mines, so it was with some risk that this assistance was offered by one of the Liverpool pilot boats.

How had they got onto the Hoyle bank? I can only assume that they mistook the Great Ormes Head for Point Lynas. They were 7 miles off the headland in the early morning in foggy weather. With limited navigational lights being shown because of the war, the mistake in identification is understandable. Then their plotted course for the Bar Light would have taken them instead onto the north east end of the West Hoyle bank.

The vessel was firmly stranded on the sandbank. The rivets started to pop as she took the strain. The crew were taken off and some attempt was made to unload some of her cargo. An eye witness report tells of the ship stuck on the Hoyle bank with its stern towards Hilbre. She kept steam up for a few days and lighters drew alongside to take off salvaged material. She was still in her peace-time colours with white upperworks and a grey hull with the funnel having the owner's house colours. In April 1941, 360 tons of sulphur were recovered. The ship became more hogged as she broke her back on the bank. Her condition deteriorated steadily and it became impractical to salvage any more of her cargo. Instead attempts were made to salvage the iron of the ship herself. However, any salvage came to a complete halt when the coaster *Maurita*, carrying coal from Point of Ayr to Lancaster, was mined in Hilbre Swash on 12 November 1941 with the loss of all 5 crew. Hilbre Swash is very near the site of the *Nestos*, so there was a real danger to the salvage vessels. By 1943 she was being used by the RAF as a target for bombing practice.

This wreck is still visible above water. From Hoylake promenade or from Hilbre Island, at low water, she can be seen with binoculars. The engine block stands proud encrusted with a thick layer of mussels. To the east lie her three boilers, while to the west are the remains of the steering quadrant looking from a distance like some huge metal mushroom. I have swum around the wreck, but the underwater visibility is essentially nil. At spring low water, there is quite extensive wreckage above water - a 'wellington boot job'.

The *Nestos* in her earlier days as the *Arabian Prince*.

The steering quadrant of the *Nestos* at low water.

Chapter 7

Wartime Coaster Losses

The importance and dangers of the trans-atlantic convoys have often been empha-
sized and dramatised. A less recognised but equally important part of the War
effort was played by the coasters that distributed cargo around the coast of Britain.
They travelled alone with at most a small gun for protection. The shipping marks
were only dimly lit and they travelled routes sometimes unswept by minesweepers. The losses of 6 vessels are described. Some of these smaller vessels lie still
fairly intact on the seabed.

After mid 1940, the censor did not allow details of ship losses to be published. So
there were no contemporary newspaper reports of the heroism or tragedy of these
wrecks. The wartime official records are far from complete, so for some wrecks very
little is known. In one case, the *Speke*, the litigation following her loss is recorded in
minute detail in Lloyds Law Reports. It also raises the question of exactly why she
was lost. Here the evidence from her wreckage clarifies the mystery surrounding
her disappearance.

Photographs of individual coasters are harder to obtain than those of larger vessels.
Coasters were so commonplace as to be overlooked in their day. I have not been
able to obtain photographs of the *Speke* or *Mancunium*.

Coasters typically had a crew of around 8: master, mate, engineer, seamen and
firemen. Although as few as 4 or 5 are reported to have crewed some vessels,
presumably because of shortage of manpower during the war. The introduction of
oil-fired engines also helped, since less manpower was needed than when coal was
burnt. Most coasters had one or two gunners aboard too. Early in the war a Lewis
gun was carried but this was of limited use against aircraft. By mid 1942, Oerlikon
guns were becoming available and they provided a more effective defence.

Gorsethorn

Steam coaster 429 tons gross, 150 ft long, 24 ft beam, 11 ft draught.
Built: Cochrane and Sons, Selby 1917.
Engines: steam triple compound, 69 rhp, single boiler.
Owners: Ribble Shipping Co.(managed W. J. Ireland), registered Liverpool.
Date of wreck: 8 Dec 1940
Location: 53^0 32.08′ N 3^0 22.13′ W
Distance from New Brighton: 13 nautical miles.
Depth at low water: 23m seabed, 25m scour, 20m to top of wreck.

The *Gorsethorn* started life as the *Jarrix* built for the Robert Rix Company who were based at Hull. Their vessels had names ending -*rix*. She was a 3 masted steel steamer designed for the East Coast coal trade. The Ribble Shipping company acquired her in 1939. Although she was lost early in the war, she is not listed among losses due to enemy action. Indeed she is reported in Lloyd's Register Wreck Returns as having foundered near the Bar Light while on a voyage from Preston to Cork with a cargo of coal. By late 1940, the censor was limiting the information published in newspapers about details of shipping losses. The only newspaper record I have been able to find is of a report of the body of a seaman wearing a lifebelt washed up on the beach at Penmaenmawr on 10 December. The body was said to have been in the water a few days and could not be identified. It is not known whether the unfortunate man was from the *Gorsethorn*.

The Hydrographic Office gives the location quoted above for her wreckage. She sank quite near the bar light and because she was in the shipping lane she has been blasted with explosives to reduce the obstacle to shipping. The bow, which is to the south, is the most prominent remaining feature. It rises about 5 metres above the scour trench. She has a boiler amidships and the stern is to the north east. The sea bed is rather silty and easily stirred up. The *Gorsethorn* lies in the no-anchoring zone near the entrance to the main shipping channel, so a quick dive keeping a good surface lookout is advisable.

Ystroom

Dutch motor coaster 400 tons gross, 198 ft long, 30 ft beam, 8 ft draught.
Built: NVC Van der Giessen & Zonen's Schps, Krimpen(Holland) 1936.
Engines: 7 Cylinder oil engines, 160 nhp, built Werkspoor NV, Amsterdam.
Owners: N.V. Stoomb. Maats., registered Amsterdam.
Date of wreck: 23 Dec 1940
Reported Location: 53^0 37′ N 3^0 25′ W

The *Gorsethorn* in her earlier days as the *Jarrix*.

The *Ystroom*.

German forces invaded the Netherlands in May 1940. Four coasters belonging to the Holland Steamboat Company decided to leave Amsterdam on 11 May. They were the *Amstelstroom*, *Vechtstroom*, *Vliestroom* and *Ijstroom*. With one hour to get ready, the ships left for Ijmuiden. Three of the captains took their families with them - including young children - which was not the usual practice. After spending the night in Ijmuiden, they sailed to Britain. The British authorities were not very welcoming to the families of the sailors since they had refused to allow families from other foreign ships to disembark. Eventually, a blind eye was turned and they were accepted.

One of these four ships was the *Ijstroom*. Her name is written *Ystroom* in English and it means the 'river Y' which is one of the rivers flowing into Amsterdam. The *Ystroom* was a relatively new vessel and she was soon at work around the coast of Britain under the command of Captain G. Speelman. Unfortunately, after only a few months, she was sunk by a mine off Liverpool. She was a small coaster with diesel engines aft and a cruiser stern. She was carrying a cargo of china clay from Teignmouth to Weston Point docks at Runcorn. All the crew were saved.

This wreck is not charted since the present position of the wreck is unknown. The reported position of loss is close to the *El Oso*.

Calcium

Steam coaster 613 tons gross, 180 ft long 28 ft wide 11 ft draught.
Built: G. Brown at Greenock 1918.
Engines: Steam triple compound (single boiler), 81 rhp, built McKie and Baxter, Glasgow.
Owners: ICI(Alkali) Ltd., registered Liverpool.
Date of wreck: 30 Dec 1940.
Location: 53^0 25.68' N 3^0 30.00' W
Distance from New Brighton: 17 nautical miles.
Depth at low water: 15m seabed, 16m scour, 12m to top of wreck.

The *Calcium* was a steam coaster owned by ICI and usually carried chemicals, particularly limestone from their quarry in North Wales to the Burn Naze Works at Fleetwood. They had a fleet of coasters with names of chemical elements: *Barium*, *Calcium*, *Sodium*, *Gallium* etc.

The *Calcium* left Fleetwood on 29 December 1940 at 21.15 in company with her sister ship the *Sodium*. They were en route for Llandulas in ballast. The crews were looking forward to getting back to their home port of Fleetwood for the New Year. The weather was reasonably good and they were making 6 knots. At 0430, when they were near Great Ormes Head, an explosion occurred under the stokehold

The *Calcium*.

The *Penrhos* in her earlier days as the *Stanley*.

about 40 metres from the bow on the starboard side. She had set off a mine. The
engine stopped immediately and there was steam everywhere from burst pipes.
The lights went out and with no steam pressure to work the whistle, no signal
could be sent to the *Sodium*. Captain Atkinson tried to investigate the damage but
hurt his leg falling down the bunker manhole. This was open on deck because
the cover had been blown off. A check was made of the crew of nine (including
one gunner for the Lewis gun carried) but the fireman James Morris could not be
found. The stokehold was full of steam and it took some time to find a way in. The
alleyway was flooded by about a metre of water as the vessel settled by the stern.
The body of the fireman was found lying under water near the starboard side of
the furnace and was brought up on deck.

The donkey pump had been blown across the engine room floor and the dynamo
had been put out of action. The wireless was not operational and there was other
serious damage. The *Sodium* had apparently heard the explosion and turned back
to help. She came alongside about 30 minutes later taking the crew aboard and
offering to tow the *Calcium*. The *Calcium* had her bow sticking in the air with
her forefoot plainly visible. The weather was freshening and the tow rope parted
several times. It proved impossible to tow her fast enough and she was sinking
lower and lower in the water. She finally listed to port and sank at about 8.20,
several miles east of the position of the mine explosion. The vessel was degaussed
and the degaussing equipment was reported to be in working order. It seems likely
that she had struck an acoustic or a contact mine, perhaps laid by a submarine.

The wreck location charted was thought at one time to be the *Lelia* and the general
layout, size and location of the wreck fits reasonably. She is about a mile south
of the North Hoyle buoy. Her bow points east and is upside down. There is a
nice swim-through here. There is a big boiler amidships and some stern ribs are
relatively upright. There is a gap between the bow and stern sections but only of
a few metres. She is relatively shallow so underwater visibility is good and there
is plenty of marine life. At times there are so many small fish that the wreck is
obscured. Another speciality of the wreck is the large conger population. I have
seen as many as three in a row in one crack at times.

More detailed investigation of the wreck shows that it is more modern. Her anchor
is still attached and looks as if it is from this century. There are signs of electric
wiring in places - not invented in Confederate times! The *Lelia* had four boilers not
one. A guide to identification is that the coaster *Calcium* is noted as being mined at
53^0 25' N 3^0 45' W but as eventually sinking at 53^0 25' N 3^0 30' W which is close to
the position of this wreck.

Mancunium

Sludge vessel 1286 tons gross, 246ft long, 38ft beam, 15 ft draught.
Built: Ferguson and Sons, Port Glasgow 1933
Engines: two 3 cylinder compound steam engines, 206 nhp, 2 single-ended boilers, twin screw.
Owners: Manchester Corporation.
Date of wreck: 15 January 1941
Location: 53^0 33.45' N 3^0 18.70' W
Distance from New Brighton: 12 nautical miles.
Depth at low water: 14m seabed, 13m to top of wreck.

This wreck has everything for the anally fixated! The *Mancunium* was a sludge vessel bringing Manchester's sewage to be dumped at sea. This practice continues and the site currently used is marked by a buoy as 'Spoil' and is close to the wreck site.

The *Mancunium* left Davyhulme Wharf, Manchester carrying a cargo of 1050 tons of sewage sludge for disposal at sea. Near her destination she was mined. The crew of 19 were all picked by two HM trawlers. At about the same time and nearby, the coaster *Karri* was also damaged by a mine. Her crew were also all picked up - by the *Mountstewart*. The MDHB salvage vessel *Vigilant* and tugs were sent to try and salvage these ships. They could not help the *Mancunium* which had sunk, but they managed to extinguish a fire on the *Karri*, put pumps aboard and get her to Liverpool.

The *Mancunium* had capsized and her bow was afloat with her stern resting on the bottom. The bow was sunk by gunfire from HMS *St. Dominica*. The wreck was marked by buoys and was dispersed in 1947. The wreck was lying bottom up with the bow pointing SE. The Admiralty Wreck Dispersal Vessels HMS *Annet* and *Fetlar* were used. They used the burial method which involved placing explosive charges along one side of the wreck to create a big trench into which the wreckage could fall. Eventually they succeeded in reducing her to lying only 2 metres above the surrounding sea bed. There is a strong magnetometer signal which helps in locating the wreck. Even so, tangled wreckage partly covered in sand and sludge is most probably what you may be able to see. For some reason, I have not got round to diving this wreck yet!

Penrhos

Steam coaster 187 tons gross, 100 ft long, 22 ft beam, 10 ft draught.
Built: W. J. Yarwood, Northwich 1904.
Engines: Steam compound 2 cylinder (one boiler), 30 rhp.
Owners: Straits Steamship Co., registered Liverpool.
Date of wreck: 1 Jan 1942
Location: 53^0 22.98' N 3^0 41.62' W
Distance from New Brighton: 24 nautical miles.
Depth at low water: 14m seabed, 17m scour, 11m to top of wreck.

The *Penrhos* was built as the *Stanley* for the Stanley Steamship Company. She was built at Northwich at the head of the Weaver navigation - quite far inland. To this day coasters still ply the Weaver, although ship building has ceased. The Stanley Steamship Company was taken over by Steam Coasters Ltd. Eventually the small coaster passed into the ownership of the Straits Steamship Company who changed her name. She was on a passage from Penmaenmawr for Liverpool on 1 January 1942 with a cargo of limestone chippings and she was seen passing Great Ormes Head. She is believed to have been sunk by a mine and her crew of four were all lost. The listed position of her wreck is 1 mile from the North Constable buoy at 243^0.

The wreck of this small coaster lies upright sticking out of the sand. Her bows are north and stern south. The current has scoured deeply around the bows and stern. Amidships her gunwales are almost level with the sea bed. She is reasonably intact and there is no obvious sign of any mine damage. Her anchor winch and loading winch are forward each side of the remains of her forecastle. She has a single hold which is now full of sand. Her rear deck houses are still in place but one can swim through easily. The single boiler can just be seen underneath. On her rear deck house roof, there is what looks like part of a gun mounting. Her propeller and rudder are mostly buried in the sand.

There is one puzzle, however. A bell bearing the legend 'Island Queen 1916' was recovered by divers from this wreck. The *Island Queen* was a 803 ton steamer with 2 boilers. She was renamed the *Foynes* in 1920 and was owned by the Limerick Steamship Company. The *Foynes* is listed as sunk in Valencia harbour in Spain by aircraft on 27 January 1939. It is hard to imagine how the bell from the *Foynes* got recycled for use on the *Penrhos*.

Speke

Steam coaster 217 tons gross, 112 ft long, 22 ft beam, 9 ft draught.
Built: Cochrane, Selby 1913.
Engines: steam compound engine (single boiler) of 55 nhp built C. D. Holmes, Hull.
Owners: Edward Nicholson, registered Liverpool.
Date of wreck: 27 Sept 1943
Location: 53^0 35.70' N 3^0 18.77' W
Distance from New Brighton: 13 nautical miles.
Depth at low water: 16m seabed, 18m scour, 12m to top of wreck.

The *Speke* was bought in 1938 by Nicholsons from Belgian owners E. Rau of Ostend. At that time her name was changed from the *Raymond*. Before that she was named *Glenmona* and owned by John Pattison of Whitehaven. She was a small steam coaster and rather than triple compound steam engines, she had the less efficient compound engines in order to save space. I have been unable to find an illustration of the *Speke* but she had a similar appearance to the *Penrhos* and *Penstone* which are both illustrated.

The *Speke* was lost on a passage from Liverpool to Preston - not a long passage by today's standards. She was loaded with a cargo of 144 tons of wood pulp from Canada in rolls and bales in the Alexandra dock on 26 and 27 September. Some 28 tons of this was carried as deck cargo on top of the hatch. She entered the Mersey via the Gladstone Lock at 7.10 pm on 27 September. Shortly after 9 pm, she reported by morse lamp to the Examination Vessel cruising in the vicinity of the Bar Lightship. The wind was moderate SSW (force 5) with rain squalls and was steadily deteriorating. She only had 10 miles to go to reach the shelter of the Ribble estuary. The *Speke* was never seen again. The bodies of her 7 crew and 2 DEMS gunners were picked up at various beaches around the west coast.

There was an inquiry to help ascertain the cause of the tragedy. Even though ships were being lost to enemy action through mines, air attack and U-boats, the lack of any wreckage suggested that these were not the cause. She was routed through a swept sea lane and no new mines could have been dropped because no enemy aircraft had been sighted since the area was swept. Another piece of evidence was that the bodies recovered showed no signs of injury (apart from the rather grisly fact that one eye was missing). What gave a clue to the most probable cause was an incident that occurred when she was being loaded with cargo. She was found to have a slight list and, when the ship's derrick was being used to transfer some bales weighing less than a ton, she developed an even greater list - of some 6^0. This suggested that she was rather unstable and that if her cargo shifted a little, she might capsize. Indeed evidence was presented at the inquiry that the cargo in the hold was stowed with sufficient empty space to have allowed such movement.

There was some uncertainty as to whether the deck cargo was securely lashed in place. It was not the case that all the cargo was put on board regardless. Indeed 124 bales were left behind in the barge from which she was loading.

Such loading practices cannot have been uncommon, so why had the *Speke* survived for so long? By this time in the war, coasters were provided with anti-aircraft defence under the Defensively Equipped Merchant Ships organisation. The gunners were naval ratings. The *Speke* had been fitted with an Oerlikon gun and heavy protection was built around the wheelhouse. These and other alterations added some 18 tons to her top weight - enough to change her stability substantially. This extra top weight was partly offset by some 8 tons of cement used to affect temporary repairs to the bottom of her hull. The combination of this additional weight added to her superstructure and the deck cargo was her undoing.

A court case was brought by the widow of one of the naval gunners claiming negligence by the stevedores who loaded the *Speke*. This investigated in great detail the loading of the bales and rolls. The judge ruled that negligence was not proved.

One can even understand why she sank where she did. Her route from Liverpool to Preston would take her out by the main Crosby channel and then around the outside of Jordan's Spit. As she passed the end of Jordan's Spit, she would alter course to the north east. The shallow spit causes steeper waves and, together with the change of course, this could have made the cargo shift a little. Then her inherent instability would make her capsize quickly. Indeed the crew had no time to launch a boat. The *Speke* carried a radio and no distress signal was received. Her two lifeboats were eventually washed ashore. No other wreckage was found at the time.

The wreck shows no sign of mine damage and the bows are facing east - the way she was heading. She is on her port side. The measurements of her hull and bar keel fit those of the *Speke* exactly. Even traces of her cargo remain. The assumptions made about her loss seem to be completely confirmed.

The *Speke* is an excellent dive. She is fairly shallow so the water is relatively sunny. Rolls of wood pulp which look like rolls of cloth are to be found in the hold. Her propeller and rudder are intact and her hull and hold are pretty much complete. The engine room at the stern is still enclosed by the hull and quarter deck. The bridge area which is at the stern has collapsed. Shoals of small fish shelter around the wreck.

The *Speke* is hard to find since she is a small wreck and quite shallow so you have to be in exactly the right area to get an echo sounder signal. She seems to lie about 100m east of the charted position given above. She is near the Jordan's Spit buoy and I find that she is 0.32 nautical miles at 090^0M from it. On one very unusual day, it was so calm that I could see the surface disturbance of the current passing over the wreck and drop the anchor by eye. Unfortunately such days are rare.

Chapter 8

Miscellaneous wreckage

There are many underwater obstructions in Liverpool Bay. The Kingfisher Charts show hundreds of 'fasteners' - places where fishing nets have been snagged by something. Some of these obstructions are also charted by the Hydrographic Office. The best marked are the Wartime Anti-aircraft Forts. Buoys mark Burbo Tower and Formby Tower. Queens Tower is marked as an obstruction. These Forts are shown in wartime photographs to have been quite substantial constructions. I have been able to locate the remains of the Formby Tower.

The concrete barge is another speciality of Liverpool Bay. Many are charted in the region just east of the wreck of the *Chagres*. Presumably this was a MDHB dumping ground. As well as concrete barges, there are quite a few large blocks of concrete or masonry here and in other parts of Liverpool Bay. Several collapsed beacons are also marked on the chart. Any of these objects is a big improvement on sand as a dive site, but none is associated with any dramatic human story.

One surprising obstruction is a fairly intact lightship. The position is close to that of the North West Lightship. This Lightship was replaced by an unmanned light in 1927. I have been able to establish that this wreck is that of the Lightship *Alarm* which was sunk in 1911.

There are also charted obstructions which are of unknown origin but which are large enough to be wrecked shipping. They were found during surveying or from trawlers catching their nets. Two are prominently marked on the hydrographic chart west of the Bar Light. They were both swept by wire to establish the maximum height of the underwater obstruction. I have dived these two wrecks and I discuss possible identification of the vessels now lying on the sea bed.

Lightship Alarm

Lightship 224 tons gross, 119 ft long, 21 ft wide, 11 ft draught.
Built: W. H. Potter and sons, Liverpool 1885.
Owners: Mersey Docks and Harbour Board.
Date of wreck: 22 August 1911.
Location: 53^0 31.35' N 3^0 30.83' W
Distance from New Brighton: 18 nautical miles.
Depth at low water: 29m seabed, 30m scour, 23m to top of wreck.

The Mersey Docks and Harbour Board took the initiative of establishing a lightship to mark the channel into Liverpool as early as 1813. This first lightship was the North West Lightship and was a converted ship. They subsequently ordered specially designed vessels as lightships. In 1911, the Mersey Docks and Harbour Board were responsible for providing 4 lightships: two outer ones (the Bar and North West Lightships) and two inner ones (the Formby and Crosby Lightships). They had 6 lightships in total, allowing one reserve for the outer stations and one for the inner stations. They had need of this reserve when the steamer *Pacuare* collided with the North West Lightship *Alarm* and sank it. Collisions between ships and lightships were quite common - their lightship *Comet* was hit and sunk three times although the *Comet* was repaired and put back in service each time.

The *Alarm* was sturdily built of iron. Her intended role was as a steam watch vessel. She could stand over wrecks in the river or bay to act as a temporary navigation warning. She also saw some service as a tender to dredging operations. In 1899, she was converted to the role of a static lightship and her boilers and engine were removed. She had a powerful clockwork operated light, a steam operated foghorn and submarine signalling apparatus. The submarine signalling was a new idea introduced in 1906 and consisted of a large bell suspended over the side in 6 metres depth which was struck rapidly by a hammer using compressed air. It was claimed that ships with suitable underwater receivers could detect the sound 15 miles away and could even tell the direction. This was only used in fog. The bell was large (150 kg) and a spare was also carried. The lightship was moored between two anchors on opposite sides with around 300 metres of chain to each.

The *Pacuare* was an Elder and Fyffes ship of 3891 tons gross. She had brought a cargo of bananas to Manchester but was unable to unload because of a strike. She then proceeded back to sea to jettison her cargo of rotten bananas. The morning was misty with a light NE wind. Around noon, she hit the Lightship on its port side with considerable force. She was over 10 times heavier than the lightship and so she pushed it along quite a way in front of her bows. The swivel connecting the Lightship to its mooring chains was broken. Luckily the Lightship's boat was ready on the starboard side hanging from the davits. All but one of the crew managed to get into the boat in the 3 minutes before the Lightship sank. The remaining crew

The North West Lightship *Alarm*.

An anti-aircraft fort in Liverpool Bay.

member was picked up from the water by this boat. There were 8 crew on the Lightship and though they lost their possessions, there were no recorded injuries. In the resulting court case, the *Pacuare* was held responsible and there was endless quibbling about the exact value to put on the loss of the *Alarm* and on the costs of providing a replacement. Her eventual replacement was also called the *Alarm* and was used as the Bar Lightship: she had a more modern appearance with a large central light fitting.

The Lightship wreck is charted as 'unknown'. On the bottom lies an upright iron vessel with a rudder but no propeller. She is of a size and shape to be a lightship. None of the superstructure remains but parts of what may be a foghorn are visible. Her bow with chain holes and anchor bollards lies to the east and her stern to the west. Part of her port side is missing but otherwise the hull is intact. Pottery which seems to be for ship's use is found on this wreck. This pottery was manufactured by Minton in 1910 and has a crest with the word 'Marine' and a wreath of leaves with a crown over an anchor inside. Rumours of the discovery of a large bell have reached me - possibly used by a lightship as a sound signal. It is almost certain that this wreck is indeed the *Alarm*.

Anti-aircraft Forts

Formby Tower: 53^0 34.45' N 3^0 13.12' W
Queens Tower: 53^0 32.68' N 3^0 17.55' W
Burbo Tower: 53^0 30.33' N 3^0 17.32' W

These anti-aircraft forts were substantial constructions, each consisting of a group of steel buildings on legs above the sea. They were towed into position and were intended to protect against aircraft dropping mines in the shipping channels. They were dismantled after the second world war so not very much may remain. Each is charted as an obstruction. There are Kingfisher 'fasteners' reported close to the position of the Formby Tower and Queens Tower so some wreckage still stands clear of the sea bed.

Formby Tower is marked by a cardinal buoy 0.1 nautical mile to the north. The seabed is sand and the visibility underwater is quite good. The depth is only 8 metres at low tide. I have searched for wreckage with a magnetometer and found a strong signal just south of the buoy. To check whether all the remaining steel is sanded in, I searched with an echo sounder and found evidence of one area with wreckage 2 metres above the seabed of sand. This should make a good shallow dive.

Queens Tower is also in an area which should be reasonable for diving, but, in a cursory search, I could find no trace of wreckage there.

Unknown A

Location: 53^0 36.00' N 3^0 29.12' W.
Distance from New Brighton: 18 nautical miles.
Depth at low water: 26m seabed, 30m scour, 20m to top of wreck.

This wreck was discovered by surveying after the War and was swept by wire to establish the exact clearance. The survey reported the wreck as lying at 145^0 and appearing to be 100 metres long. This wreck is listed by the MDHB and Hydrographic Office as 'Unknown'. It lies somewhat west of the charted wreck of the *Munster*. Indeed some divers believe that this wreck is part of the *Munster* although that is not confirmed by the detailed wreckage lying on the seabed.

From diving on the wreck, I estimate that she lies north-south with her bows south. Her bow section is fairly intact and is upside down. Amidships and the stern are more broken up but there are 6m vertical sections at the stern. A large mast lies to the west amidships. Part of a gun has been found near the stern. There are remains of engine components and one boiler is prominent at the north west corner of the wreck. This is a boiler which has a size typical of boilers found on coasters. There appears to be a second similar boiler underneath wreckage nearby. Overall, the size of the wreckage suggests a ship of around 1000 tons. The wreck has a variety of marine life with many congers. The vertical plates are festooned with huge orange and white plumose anenomes. It is a very attractive dive site.

From the state of corrosion of the hull, I estimate that she is of Second World War vintage. The *Stanleigh* and *Ystroom* are the only unlocated Second World War wrecks I am aware of. The *Ystroom* had diesel engines - so no boiler. This leaves the *Stanleigh* as a candidate: she had two boilers. She is reported to have been bombed 12 miles from the Bar Light so it is surprising that she ended up only 6.5 miles away from the Bar. However, several other wrecks are now located equally far from their position reported in wartime. The overall size of the wreck and the fact that the engine machinery is all located at the stern both fit the *Stanleigh*. It will be interesting to find more definite evidence about the identity of this wreck.

Unknown B

Location: 53^0 32.73' N 3^0 23.70' W
Distance from New Brighton: 14 nautical miles.
Depth at low water: 22m seabed, 23m scour, 18m to top of wreck.

This underwater obstruction was reported in 1946 during surveying. It was subsequently swept by wire to establish that the wreck was no shallower than 15.7 metres above chart datum (lowest astronomical tide). The site is mentioned in Zanelli's 'Unknown Shipwrecks around Britain' as a possible dive site. He suggests that the wreck is likely to be of Second World War origin but may possibly be covered in sand by now.

After several attempts, I have located this wreck and dived it. The wreck is a substantial iron vessel which is lying on its side. She is on her port side with bows facing north. The deck is vertical and, in some places, rises over 4 metres from the scour trench. Most of the wreck is buried beneath the sea bed and no engine components are visible. She has a vertical bow and a counter stern. The size of the wreck is consistent with that of a large coaster - being about 60 metres long. Only the starboard side of the wreck protrudes from the sea bed and the hull is fairly intact except for a break near the centre. There is some fishing net draped around the break area. The wreck is covered in large white and orange plumose anenomes. This part of Liverpool Bay is quite silty - one should try to avoid contact with the bottom to keep underwater visibility reasonable. The wreck has some overhanging parts so care is needed when diving in poor visibilty to avoid unwittingly entering the wreck. This area is also a no-anchoring zone.

From the state of corrosion of the hull, I estimate that she is over 50 years old. Quite a lot of broken crockery, bottles and jars are lying on the sea bed near the wreck - although these may come from some later dumping since they do not seem to be very old. The *Stanleigh* and *Ystroom* are the only unlocated Second World War wrecks I am aware of. I believe that the *Stanleigh* is a candidate for 'Unknown A'. This leaves the *Ystroom* as a possibility. Only the approximate position of sinking of the *Ystroom* is available: 53^0 37' N 3^0 25' W. That position is close to the *El Oso* and about 4 miles from 'Unknown B'. The shape of the hull of the coaster *Ystroom* does not seem to be consistent with that of this wreck.

Another possibility is that this wreck is much earlier and is the *Lelia*. As explained in the chapter on confederate ships, the *Lelia* may well have foundered near the present position of the Bar Light. She was a shallow draught paddle steamer of 640 tons gross which was 250 ft long. The overall shape of the hull of 'Unknown B' is very similar to that of a shallow draught paddle steamer. There is some sign of what may be a part of the paddle wheel cover at the midships break. It will be interesting to make a positive identification - particularly from the engine components - since the *Lelia* had 4 boilers.

Chapter 9

Recent wrecks

Despite modern safety equipment there are still shipwrecks in Liverpool Bay. Collisions between ships in fog and collisions with an underwater obstruction were the causes of these wrecks. The most recent was the *Ardlough* in 1988. The stories of the loss of the *Berwyn* and *Penstone* are recounted. Fortunately the crews of the *Berwyn* and *Ardlough* were all saved. Only the loss of the *Penstone* was a human tragedy.

Penstone

Steam coaster 267 tons gross, 120 ft long, 22 ft beam, 9 ft draught.
Built: Manchester Drydock Co, Ellesmere Port 1926.
Engines: Steam compound 2 cylinder (one boiler), 52 nhp.
Owners: Zillah Shipping and Carrying Co., registered Liverpool.
Date of wreck: 31 July 1948
Location: 53^0 29.86' N 3^0 37.48' W
Distance from New Brighton: 21 nautical miles.
Depth at low water: 34m seabed, 35m scour, 25m to top of wreck.

The Zillah company was managed by W. A. Savage and had a fleet of coasters. Their business started by carrying roadstone from the quarries at Penmaenmawr. After the first World War, they traded more generally and moved their headquarters to Liverpool. The *Penstone* was named after Penmaenmawr *stone*. She was a small coaster of rather old fashioned design. Her builder's plans are available in the Merseyside Maritime Museum.

On 29 July 1948, she left Coburg dock, Liverpool with a cargo of grain for Barrow. She then sailed light to Penmaenmawr to load 220 tons of granite chippings for Preston. She left Penmaenmawr on the North Wales coast at 8 am on 31 July. There was thick fog with visibility of 40 yards. Just south of the North West Light, she heard the Norwegian MV *Villanger* approaching. The 4484 ton ship struck her just forward of the bridge, nearly cutting her in two. She sank fast. A crew of 5 and the master's 10 year old son were on board. Those off watch were below and had no chance. The rest were thrown into the water. Only the mate and second engineer survived to be picked up by a boat from the *Villanger* a half hour later. There was no sign of any other survivors. The master John Stevenson (age 36), his son Norman (age 10), his brother Albert (age 32) and the chief engineer Daniel Banks (age 64) were lost.

She is upright on the sea bed and fairly intact. Her stern is the highest part and lies to the north west.

Berwyn

Motor coaster 696 tons gross, 195 ft long, 30 ft beam, 12 ft draught.
Built: Norrkoping Varv. & Verks., Norrkoping, Sweden 1949.
Engines: Oil 4 cylinders, 660 bhp, built Nydqvist & Holm.
Owners: Effluent Services Ltd., registered Liverpool.
Date of wreck: 15 February 1973
Location: 53^0 32.2' N 3^0 14.2' W
Distance from New Brighton: 10 nautical miles.
Depth at low water: 8m seabed, 6m to top of wreck.

The *Berwyn* had lived a busy life changing names frequently since she was built in Sweden as the *Margit Reuter*. She became the *Sylvia, Jill J* and *Mabelstan* in succession. As the *Mabelstan* she was owned by Southern Tanker and Bunkering, based on Guernsey. Her final change of name to *Berwyn* was only a year before she met her end. She was a motor tanker, taking industrial waste out to sea for disposal. On the 15 February she was outward bound from Liverpool and was just passing the end of the shipping channel when she struck an underwater obstacle. Presumably she had cut the corner too finely and had caught the western end of the north training wall. These training walls are stone and concrete and are designed to keep the main channel deep by forcing the tide to flow between them.

She started taking in water fast and developed a serious list. The crew of 7 were taken off by the MDHC salvage vessel *Vigilant* which was passing. They leapt from the *Berwyn* just as her decks were awash. The rescue was just in time since the *Berwyn* sank minutes later. She went down to the North of the Q2 buoy which is out of the main shipping lane and sank on her side lying $010^0/190^0$. She was reduced by explosives during a salvage operation. Since she is relatively shallow, the strong seas have smashed her further.

The *Penstone*.

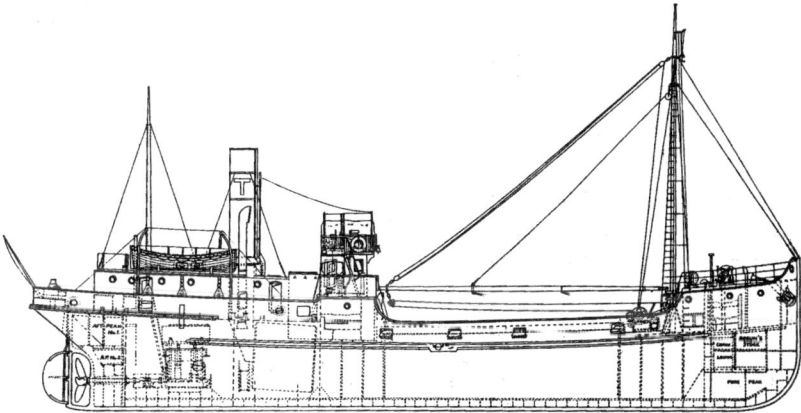

Plans of the *Penstone*.

Even though she lies quite close to the muddy Mersey channel, the wreck is shallow and underwater visibility is a few feet at times. The bottom is firm sand with bits of solid wreckage embedded in it. Another wreck, the *Dunmail* lies in a similar location and it is hard to be sure which wreckage is which. The *Dunmail* was a 1337 ton steamship that grounded during a gale on 10 August 1873. She too was reduced by blasting.

Ardlough

Container ship 998 tons gross, 285 ft long, 48 ft beam, 15 ft draught.
Built: Schlichting Werft, Travemunde, East Germany 1968.
Engines: 6 cylinder 2500 bhp, built Keil, Germany.
Registered: Antigua/Barbuda.
Date of wreck: 26 September 1988
Location: 53^0 34.97' N 3^0 50.36' W
Distance from New Brighton: 29 nautical miles.
Depth at low water: 40m seabed, 20m to top of wreck.

The *Ardlough* was built in East Germany as the *Barbel Bolten* for a West German company based in Hamburg. She was strongly built - her construction is described as 'ice strengthened' and she had a bulbous bow. She was sold to Holland in 1973 and renamed the *Theano*. After 6 years, she returned to West German ownership as the *Ekenis*. It appears that she was under charter to Coastal Containers, a Liverpool company, and she made regular journeys from Liverpool to Belfast. She was renamed the *Ardlough* in 1988. Her master was German and the crew of 9 were Philippino.

She had left Garston docks during the night carrying a cargo of coal, steel and newsprint. Soon after leaving, she began leaking in the hold and radioed for help. The leak may have been caused by her striking a lock wall on leaving Garston. She began to sink in rough seas off the North Wales coast. Her master and crew were taken off by RAF helicopter in the early hours of the morning. The deck cargo of 12 containers broke loose when she sank and were scattered widely by the gale force winds and strong tidal currents of Liverpool Bay. The containers were a considerable hazard to shipping until they in turn sank.

This wreck lies in deep water so care is needed when diving. She is pretty much intact at present. She is upright and lies east - west. In late 1993 she was swept clear by wire to 15.8 metres minimum depth. A South Cardinal buoy marking the wreck was placed nearby to the south.

The *Berwyn*.

The *Ardlough* arriving in the Mersey the day before she was lost.

Chapter 10

Diving Liverpool Bay

Where to dive

Liverpool Bay is the name of the sea area covering the approaches to Liverpool. Up to about 20 miles from Liverpool the sea is less than 20 metres deep at low tide. There are sand banks either side of the shipping channels into the Mersey and into the Dee. The sea bed is sand and can shift. There are strong tidal currents with a maximum tidal height difference of over 10 metres at Liverpool. Because of the strong currents (5 knots) the water in the estuaries is a muddy brown - looking like tea. To get reasonable visibility under water, one has to go further out. Even 20 miles out currents can be 2 knots but they are less on neap tides and drop completely around high water and low water. The best opportunity for diving is low water neap tides - these occur around midday which is convenient. Neap tides, which have a tidal difference of as little as 5 metres, occur every fortnight. At low water neaps, there is often 5 metre visibility and at times I have experienced 15 metres. The low water depths given in earlier sections refer to low water neap tides. The deeper wrecks are rather dark and a torch is essential - but with a torch 5 metre visibility is common. Some of the wrecks have a collection of angler's monofilament lines complete with hooks and sinkers. A scissors is a useful dive accessory.

With its sandy sea bed, most of Liverpool Bay is rather unexciting to dive unless you are a marine biologist. The marine life is very different on the wrecks. They are covered in orange and white plumose anemones and have abundant fish life - pollack, bib, ling, and conger eels. There are lots of edible crabs and plenty of lobster too. So the diver should try to find an area with something to provide a base for this marine life. Aside from wrecks themselves, concrete blocks, masonry deposits and stony patches can be found and they provide a good dive. As well as fish, Liverpool Bay is also home to a large seal colony. On the South East corner of the West Hoyle sandbank there are often over 100 grey seals to be found resting at low tide. These seals feed quite widely and I have often seen one when anchored near a wreck site. I have unfortunately never yet met one under water.

The wrecks which lie in the shipping channels have all been reduced by explosives by the Mersey Docks and Harbour Board. So they look more like a scrap yard than a ship. Some of the smaller wrecks are still fairly intact - the *Speke*, *Penstone*, *Penrhos* and *Lightship*. The deeper wrecks such as the *Chagres* and *Dublin* are also more complete. The marine life is excellent on all of them - it is the wreck hunters who might prefer a ship-shaped wreck. The oldest wrecks have mostly been overtaken by the shifting sand banks - particularly wooden wrecks. Nevertheless some historic vessels may be dived - the *City of Brussels* and *Ocean Monarch* in particular. Most of the large wrecks date from a spate of sinkings by mines in the opening months of the 1939-45 War: the *Chagres, El Oso, Counsellor, Cairnross, Dosinia* and *Munster*. Details of wreck dives are given in each section. All wrecks in principle belong to someone - often an insurance company which has written off the loss. Though taking small souvenirs is tolerated, any substantial salvage needs the agreement of the owner. The Receiver of Wrecks can assist with arrangements.

A programme is currently under way to identify and visit as many of the wrecks in Liverpool Bay as possible. The motivation is to improve the chances of finding any historic vessels. Among the targets are the *Lelia* and *Resurgam*. This operation is being coordinated by Brian Atkin, the BSAC East Cheshire area coach, who can be contacted on 051 356 8745.

Another recent development (1994) is that work is underway on oil and gas production platforms in Liverpool Bay. They will be connected to each other and to the North Wales coast by underground pipelines. There will be an exclusion zone around each platform and anchoring near the pipelines will be discouraged. It is hoped that none of the wreck sites will become inaccessible.

When to dive

The Irish sea is fairly shallow with strong currents so quite steep seas can build up. There is a long fetch for any wind direction from south west round to north in Liverpool Bay. This lack of shelter to such directions increases the wave height. Thus settled weather is needed since in anything over force 4, the Bay gets rough. Wind against tide aggravates matters and causes nasty steep seas. Even so, it is possible to find calm days right through the year. The sea temperature is reasonable even in winter - with a dry suit.

Weather information is available from the Irish Sea area of the shipping forecast on Radio 4, the TV weather reports and also the Irish shipping forecast on 567 metres medium wave at 0633, 1253, 1823 and 2355.

Tidal information is the other ingredient needed for planning dives. Liverpool tide tables giving times and heights of high and low water are produced by Lavers and are available in dive and boat shops around the Liverpool area. Liverpool is a standard port and is in all Almanacs (such as MacMillan). The high tide times are very close to Dover so can be found in many newspapers. Those high tides near midday will be springs while those near 6.00 will be neap tides - this information on tidal heights is needed to estimate the strength of currents.

Although tidal atlases give a picture of currents at each hour throughout the Irish sea they are not very detailed. More accurate information comes from the 'tidal diamonds' on the charts. They give hourly information for selected locations on the direction and speed of the current for spring and for neap tides. Roughly this amounts to diveable conditions (less than a knot of current) for two hours either side of low water at neaps. This is long enough to allow two dives at low water slack if one arrives early enough. Ideally, you should plan to arrive on site two or three hours before low water neaps.

How to get there

There are several useful Admiralty charts - number 1978 is the most appropriate and covers the region as far as Great Ormes Head and Southport. The buoyed channel into Liverpool is shown on number 1951 and the Dee Estuary on number 1953. The Kingfisher charts list obstructions reported by fishing vessels in the area with their Decca positions - a good source of potential new wreck sites. The latest Kingfisher charts also give latitude and longitude. These charts can be obtained from Chart Agents such as Dubois, McCullum and Phillips in Covent Garden, Liverpool or from some local chandlers.

For those who intend to go wreck diving in their own boats, I give some navigation guidance. The wrecks are often out of sight of land and some 10 to 20 miles from the launch site. Boats must be seaworthy and equipped with adequate safety measures. Travelling in pairs is an excellent strategy for inflatables. Because of the amount of commercial shipping, it is important to have a radar reflector as well as a large A flag. Liverpool coastguard look after the area and it is worth calling them on 16 (then changing to 67) on VHF to inform them of the start of a boat trip. Their phone number is 051 931 3341.

Except for the *El Oso* which lies close to a prominent buoy, the other wrecks need accurate navigational electronics: Decca or GPS. The charted latitude and longitude is given for the wrecks listed. These can be used for GPS navigation provided the correct chart convention is selected. I quote latitude and longitude in the OSGB36 system used on British Admiralty charts. Many GPS sets use the WGS84 system and these positions will need to be moved 0.09 minutes east and 0.01 minutes south. A good check (since it does not move) is the beacon at the end of the groyne just north west of the Rock Lighthouse off New Brighton. This is charted as 53^0 26.74' N 3^0 2.70' W. For Decca navigation, the Decca lane information as used by the older professional Decca sets is excellent for finding again a previous spot. What is less easy is to relate these lane values to latitude and longitude because of the quite large fixed errors that occur in Liverpool Bay. This means that Decca navigators that give latitude and longitude readings will be off by a fixed amount, which can be hundreds of metres. This can be checked by comparing the position of charted beacons or buoys. Since Decca is less accurate close to shore, a good check is, for instance, the Bar Light which is charted at 53^0 22.00' N 3^0 20.90' W. Once a Decca set has been calibrated, then quite accurate Decca location is possible, particularly in summer around midday when interference is least.

Launch sites for trailered boats exist in several locations. The slips on the Wirral require a 'foreshore permit' to be obtained beforehand by post from the Leisure Services Department (there is no charge - they are in Hamilton St., Birkenhead L41 5DN, phone 051 647 2366). They will also send you a list of available launching slips. The slip at New Brighton is the most popular and is usable at any state of the tide. This is a concrete slip down to firm sand. Another useful concrete slip on the Wirral is at Meols (Dovepoint Road at east end of Hoylake promenade) which is usable 2 hours either side of high water. There is also a quite well protected concrete/wooden slip at Tranmere which is usable at all tide heights. The most protected launch into the Mersey is from a totally sheltered slip into Liverpool Marina (Coburg Dock) from which access to the Mersey can be made 2 hours either side of high water through the lock (there is a charge - the Marina is on 051 708 5228). Possible alternative launching sites are from the beach at Southport or from slipways along the North Wales coast at Prestatyn, Rhos or Conway.

From the launch site the charts will indicate any sand banks to be avoided on the way to the site chosen. From New Brighton, the easiest route is along the well buoyed shipping channel. On either side of this channel are 'training walls' which are blocks of stone that show at low water. Avoid them.

Once arrived on site, an echo sounder is needed to make positive identification of the wreck. Many wrecks have 'scour trenches'. These are on either side of the wreck where the sea bed is a metre or more deeper than the surrounding flat level. They are a useful guide to wreck location. One further warning - there are some pretty impressive 'sand waves' in Liverpool Bay which show pronounced steps on the echo sounder. They are very boring to dive I can assure you. So look for further evidence before you jump in. A magnetometer is a useful device too, since most of the wrecks are iron. Again some wrecks are almost completely sanded in - a magnetometer finds these too but doesn't tell you to take a spade or a JCB!

Boat charters are available from Liverpool and the North Wales coast. Many boats predominantly take out anglers who are prepared to go in any weather. Diving in substantial waves is unpleasant and dangerous. Thus be sure that any charter deal specifies what happens if the weather is too rough for safe diving. Boats currently taking divers from Liverpool include *Baccardee* and *Excelsior* (contact Chris Norton 0831 262 641) and *Dainty Lady* (contact Ron 051 678 9967), from Rhyl *Huntress* (contact Eddy Ward 0745 88 9419) and from Rhos on Sea *Rose* (contact John Povah 0745 33 1395). The Liverpool boats usually pick up divers in the Mersey at the steps alongside Albert Dock car park. They go out over low water and return some 6 to 12 hours later.

Bibliography

Lloyds Register of Shipping 1840-1990.
Lloyds Weekly Casualty Records.
Lloyds War Loss records, volume I - III.
British Vessels lost at sea 1914-1918, 1939-1945, Admiralty.
Dictionary of Disasters at Sea during the age of Steam, C. Hocking.
Lloyd's List Law Reports.
Liverpool Shipwreck and Humane Society, Annual Reports.
Disasters at Sea, M. O. Watson.
Liverpool Daily Post, Echo, Mercury and Courier.
London Illustrated News.
Mersey Docks and Harbour Board Records, Merseyside Maritime Museum.
Mersey, (Mersey Docks and Harbour Board journal).
Steam Coasters and Short Sea Traders, C. V. Waine.
British Coasting 1939-1945, The Official Story, HMSO.
Cambrian Coasting, R. S. Fenton.
Shipwrecks around Britain, Leo Zanelli.
Unknown Shipwrecks around Britain, Leo Zanelli.
Shipwrecks of North Wales, Ivor Wynne Jones.
Merchant Fleets in Profile, Duncan Holmes.
The Blue Riband of the Atlantic, Tom Hughes.
Passenger Liners of the Western Ocean, C. Vernon Gibbs.
Liverpool Shipping: a Short History, George Chandler.
The Harrison Line, F. E. Hyde.
The Bowring Story, David Keir.
Pride of the Princes, N. L. Middlemess.
Jack Billmeir - Merchant Shipowner, P. M. Heaton.
Irish Passenger Steamship Services, vol. I and II, D. B. McNeil.
The B & I Line, Hazel P. Smyth.
Clyde and other Coastal Steamers, C. L. D. Duckworth and G. E. Langmuir.
West Coast Steamers, C. L. D. Duckworth and G. E. Langmuir.
Across the Irish Sea; Belfast - Liverpool Shipping, Robert C. Sinclair.
Ships of the Isle of Man Steam Packet Company, Fred Henry.
Island Lifeline, Connery Chappell.
Liverpool Bay Lightships 1813-1913, J. W. Gracey, Eng. Soc. Trans., vol. 35.
Father of the Submarine, The Life of Rev. George Garrett Pasha, W. S. Murphy.
Garrett's Submarine Torpedo Boat, Engineer 1882.
The Quest for Gt. Britain's first Submersible, the Resurgam, Sydney Wignall, Cymru a'r Mor, vol. 3.
The Secret Service of the Confederate States in Europe, James D. Bullogh.